BANS, JAILS AND SHAMELESS LIES

Copyright © Fréderike Geerdink
Book design Edwin Smet
Final editing Barry Crooks

ISBN 978-90-823641-8-7

www.evatasfoundation.com

BANS, JAILS AND SHAMELESS LIES

Translated by Rohan Minogue

FRÉDERIKE GEERDINK

CENSORSHIP IN TURKEY

EVATASFOUNDATION

Amsterdam 2016

CONTENTS

MURDERED JOURNALISTS

FOREWORD

While writing this booklet, I frequently had to think about my fellow-journalists in Turkey doing their utmost to report on Turkey's day-to-day reality for the benefit of their readers and viewers. About those staff and freelance journalists working in newsrooms or doing their work with mud on their boots in the cities, towns and villages and in the country's fields, valleys and mountains. The more I progressed, the more I had the feeling that I was not doing them justice. Are things really as terrible for the media in Turkey as I have described? After all, the newspapers do also carry good articles, and there is an incredible number of journalists who take their calling seriously and would never write up a lie. It is not all bad, is it?

No, things are not all bad. But this booklet is not an exposition of Turkey's media landscape. It is intended to provide an understanding of the complex topic of the suppression of press freedom in Turkey. By now everyone knows that there are many journalists in Turkey behind bars on account of their work and that President Erdogan has the media in his increasingly tight grip. How has this come about? What are the mechanisms at play in the press and in politics that have reduced journalism to such a miserable condition in a country that many see as democratic after all?

These mechanisms are not discussed that often. Attention to press freedom in Turkey is frequently paid at case level in articles and reports, or, in other words: a case where a journalist, newspaper or TV station has got into difficulties is discussed, and some background is provided. There is no room in most of the articles for the full picture. No wonder, as the full picture is complex and lies deeply anchored in the structures of the Turkish state and business life. This cannot be explained in a paragraph or two. President Erdogan has heaped up restrictions on press freedom to an unheard of level, but he has been able to do that only because the Turkish political system by definition does not provide room for a free press. The more respect for my fellow journalists who strive to fight against the patterns of restricted journalistic freedom in Turkey every day, using their pens, cameras and microphones, along with all the associated risks. My dear fantastic colleagues, your work is being seen.

Journalists working for newspapers supporting the government did not want to talk to me for this booklet. I have been in touch with Ceren Kenar of Türkiye but despite initial interest in an interview she stopped getting back to me. I emailed Markan Esayan of Yeni Safak but didn't get a reply. Merve Sebnem of Sabah answered my request but said she didn't trust me so refused an interview. Kurtulus Tayiz of Aksam said he prefers to express his opinions only in his columns and not in interviews. TheKebabAndCamel.com, a website scrutinizing foreign newspapers over their Turkey coverage to which also pro-government journalists are attached, replied to personal twitter messages but didn't want to cooperate.

Neither the AKP government of Prime Minister Davutoglu nor a representative of the government or of President Erdogan is quoted directly in this booklet. The Turkish government does not often react favourably to requests for interviews, and comments on topical issues primarily in speeches, during press conferences or at gatherings where only journalists working for the media on the government side are welcome.

Added to this is that I got into difficulties in Turkey because of my work as a journalist. At the beginning of September 2015, I was put on the plane to Amsterdam under police supervision, following nine years as correspondent in Turkey, the last three as the sole foreign journalist in Diyarbakir, the Kurdish city in the south-east. I was detained while doing my work in the Yüksekova district on the Iranian border. I have been banned from entering the country for the time being. According to the Turkish authorities, I represent a threat to national order, security and health. They will not speak to me.

Prime Minister Davutoglu did speak to the Dutch public broadcaster NOS in February 2015. The Turkish prime minister was in the Netherlands (which held the EU presidency from January to June 2016) for discussions on the refugee crisis, and the NOS touched on the issue of press freedom in the interview. Turkey correspondent Lucas Waagmeester suggested to the prime minister that the media in Turkey were under pressure and that he had also heard that Turkish and foreign journalists saw it that way.

Davutoglu answered: 'What did you experience? Was there any pressure on you? Whenever I ask any journalist 'Did you face any problem?' they always say 'My colleagues did'. But I want to see someone who had really a problem of freedom of press in Turkey. Look, it is very clear. Turkey is a democratic country. Rule of law is there. Like in the Netherlands, like in all European countries. Last year you observed there were two general elections in Turkey. And I am sure you will admit that during these elections there has been heavy criticism against the government by the opposition, and also by newspapers, and other media. And four out of five of the highest circulation newspapers were not supportive of the government. And in the biggest circulation newspapers, on TV and everywhere, there was freedom of expression, freedom of the press. And this has been observed by international observers as well. So there has not been any limitation regarding freedom of expression.'

Judge for yourself.

Fréderike Geerdink
Leiden, March 2016

NAMIK TARANCI
(1955-1992)

Namık Taranci was working as a reporter in Diyarbakir, the city where he was born, for the investigative quarterly Gercek (Reality) when he was shot and killed on the street in 1992. His wife Derman related the circumstances during the days immediately before and after his death to the independent news portal bianet. org: 'Not long before his death, Namik began to receive threats by phone and he was followed. He didn't want to say anything, but I saw that there were people hanging around our house. We were under great pressure, like everyone else at the time. Living in the shadow of weapons undermines one's psychological health.'

She continued: 'That morning Namık went to the court buildings to see whether there was any news. I was at home with our little boy of three. I had dozed off, but was woken by the sound of rifle shots. I looked out of the window, but saw nothing. Then the doorbell rang. It was one of the neighbours, who said: "Your husband has been shot." I ran outside. Namık was lying on the road in a pool of blood with two plainclothes police officers standing over him. They gathered up the cartridges and then left.'

Derman Taranci relates how the funeral was anything but peaceful: 'They wouldn't leave us alone at the cemetery. They harassed us, and a number of people were detained. Namık was buried under conditions of complete panic.'

For two years the identity of the murderers was unknown, until the murder came up in the 1994 trial of Cemal Tutar, a member of the Hezbollah group that carried out political murders on behalf of the Turkish state, mainly of Kurds. Tutar was not present at the trial but was detained years later in 2000 during an anti-Hezbollah operation in Istanbul. Tutar made a statement that another person had given the order to murder Taranci and that he himself had been responsible for planning it. He also revealed who pulled the trigger and who was the lookout.

In a mass trial of Hezbollah suspects held in 2009, Tutuk was convicted and sentenced to life in prison. He appealed, and because he had been in jail since 2000 – and so for longer than 10 years without final conviction – he was released in 2011. When a court confirmed the life sentence a few days after he was released and issued an arrest warrant, Tutar could not be found. He is still at large.

Mustafa Demir, the man who fired the fatal shots, is serving a life prison term. Abdülkadir Selçuk, who was the lookout, is said to have been murdered. Isa Altsoy, the man who reportedly ordered the murder, is still on the run.

Namık Taranci, who completed his studies at the literature faculty of Gazi University in Ankara, and his wife Derman had been married for four years and had a three-year-old son. Taranci was known to the state security services. He was detained following the 1980 coup and spent six years in the prison in Diyarbakir, which was notorious at the time.

CHAPTER 1

CAN DÜNDAR: 'NOBODY WANTS THE MEDIA TO BE CALM AND OBJECTIVE ANY MORE'

Security is tight at the entrance to the newspaper Cumhuriyet. A high fence, a guardhouse at the gate in the fence, another guardhouse at the entrance to the building, a bag check just inside the hallway. The office of Can Dündar, one of Turkey's best known journalists and Cumhuriyet's current editor, is on the top floor. Does he have his own personal security? 'That has been offered to me, but I declined,' he says. 'I have to be protected not by the state, but from the state.'

It is mid-August 2015 and the large TV on the wall of Dündar's office is on with the sound turned off. Coalition talks launched following the 7 June elections are on the point of ending without an outcome, and Dündar keeps one eye on the screen. Nevertheless, the news does not appear to distract him from what he has to say. Expressing himself tersely and pointedly, he says: 'I do not feel like a journalist any more. As a journalist you follow up on a story, you maintain a wide network, and you write a balanced article. But we no longer have any links to the ruling party, the AKP. The AKP wants to get rid of Cumhuriyet, and we want to get rid of the AKP. It's war, and in a war journalism cannot be done properly.'

The war between the AKP and Cumhuriyet (which means 'Republic') broke out in earnest at the end of May 2015. The newspaper had got hold of video footage showing trucks from Turkey's intelligence service MIT on their way to the Syrian border. These trucks had previously, in early 2014, been in the news when the military police stopped and searched them at the behest of a public prosecutor. The AKP government rapidly intervened, and the trucks were allowed to proceed, with the result that rumours that they were involved in transporting weapons remained unconfirmed. Tayyip Erdogan, still prime minister of Turkey at the start of 2014, swore that they were transporting aid intended for Turkmen living in Syria, an ethnic group closely related to the Turks.

Cumhuriyet's scoop put paid to that story. The images revealed that under the packages of plasters and boxes of bandages and medicines there was something completely different hidden: artillery shells, mortar bombs and ammunition for automatic weapons.

The newspaper published the images online and carried photographs in the print edition under the headline: Look, the weapons that Erdogan said did not exist.

Erdogan pulled out all the stops to limit the damage. Through the courts – he has the judiciary fully under his control – he imposed a ban on publishing the images and access to the websites showing the images was blocked. And he vowed: 'Those responsible for making the news public will pay a high price.' In response to this, the newspaper's journalists published a front page showing the photographs and signatures of the editorial staff, along with the declaration that they all took responsibility for the scoop and wished to be pursued legally along with their editor. The state prosecutors focussed on two editors, editor-in-chief Can Dündar and Erdem Gül, the head of Cumhuriyet's bureau in the capital Ankara. In the end, the two were detained on 26 November 2015 and at the time of writing were still being held under suspicion of espionage and publishing state secrets.

Can Dündar and Erdem Gül were released in the very early hours of Friday 26 February 2016. Turkey's Constitutional Court had ruled that their detention was violating their rights. The court case against them continues. President Erdogan has stated that he does not accept nor respect the Court's ruling.

During the interview three months before their arrest, Dündar showed the front pages: the one with the scoop and the one showing the editorial staff taking joint responsibility for the revelations. Dündar: 'Actually, I hate the fact that we have ended up in this war. It's an unequal struggle as well. But I'm not giving up; we have to assert the power of journalism. I have to fight, with my pen.'

Born in 1961, Dündar began his journalistic career in 1979, while he was still studying, at the magazine Yanki, which no longer exists. The following year, on 12 September 1980, a military coup was carried out, and the press, which had been reasonably free until then, was subjected to close controls. Yanki, Dündar relates, had good connections with the army and was not targeted: 'And I was just a student and starting out as a journalist, so they were not going for me. But a lot of other media were banned, and many journalists were detained.' He recalls that at the time the army disseminated telexes to the media with binding instructions on what had to be published and more particularly what could not. Dündar: 'If you wrote the wrong thing, they came to confiscate that issue of the newspaper, or they closed it down completely.'

He decided that he no longer wanted to work in this way, resigned and concentrated on his studies, for a time at the London School of Journalism and at the Political Science faculty at a university in Ankara. Only afterwards, in 1988, did he return to journalism, working for TV and various magazines.

Referring to journalism in the years before the coup, he says: 'At the time, Turkey was ruled mostly by coalition governments, which automatically meant that no one party ever had too much power or was able to apply severe pressure on the press. Moreover, the constitution from the 1960s was still in force, which stipulated unambiguously that the press was free.'

The constitution introduced by the military in 1982 put an end to press freedom, and that constitution, while frequently amended, is still in force. Since then basic freedoms have been restricted with a whole series of provisions and exceptions that also undermine press freedom. Article 28 of the Turkish constitution says: 'The press is free and shall not be censored.' This is followed by a whole series of reasons why press freedom may indeed be restricted, namely if national and public safety and public order are at stake, or the basic characteristics of the republic and the indivisible integrity of the state and its borders are under threat. Press freedom may also be restricted if a crime or the publication of state secrets may thereby be prevented, if the reputation or the rights and private sphere of others are thereby protected, if professional secrets as described under the law are endangered, and if the proper functioning of the courts is under threat. Away with freedom of the press.

_ 'The men of the AKP have become the generals'

'The strict censorship after the coup lasted for three years,' Dündar says. 'The censorship under the AKP government has now lasted 13 years.' Although he would be the last to say that the press was free again after 1983. It was not, and many journalists paid the price with their lives, mainly Kurdish journalists working for banned Kurdish media, but also for instance investigative journalist Ugur Mumcu of Cumhuriyet, who was murdered in Ankara in 1993 (see page XX). 'During those years journalists paid a heavier price, now the pressure is much broader than at that time. Every journalist is subject to it now, every newspaper is under pressure. Many of my colleagues have bid farewell to journalism, or they have gone to work for government newspapers so as to have the pressure lifted. Eighty per cent of the media are under the direct control of the government.'

Many liberals in Turkey were full of hope when the AKP came to power 13 years ago. The AKP appeared to be pro-reform and determined on EU membership, and therefore on democratisation. Dündar: 'I did not share that hope. I believe in the separation of powers, but in Turkey this is not entrenched in the system. If a country is not ruled in accordance with democratic principles and has no tradition of civil participation, then it is dangerous if only one party is in power. This single party wants to get everything under its control: police, army, universities, the justice system and the press.'

The AKP dealt with the army's power in the first years of its rule – something that was seen by many as a victory for democracy. Dündar: 'But now the men of the AKP have become the generals. The repression is the same.'

Dündar believes that every sentence written in Cumhuriyet is closely examined by the public prosecutors: 'And that results in three or four new charges every week. Don't ask me how many court cases are now pending against Cumhuriyet. I wouldn't be able to tell you. Whenever I have to appear in court yet again to explain that an article really is journalism, I hear from the prosecutors that they see it as defamation of the president. So it continues, and all these cases drag on for years.' Most of the cases concern the MIT trucks and allegations of corruption levelled at many senior AKP officials, including Erdogan himself. Articles on the Kurdish question also cause difficulties for the newspaper, and there is a case pending because Cumhuriyet dared to publish the Charlie Hebdo cartoon of the prophet Mohammed.

Is there still good journalism in Turkey? 'No,' answers Dündar, without having to think. 'Even Cumhuriyet can no longer do that. Even we are unable to publish any balanced stories. All journalism has become political instead of social. And it couldn't be otherwise in the current climate. Once a society is as polarised as Turkey is at the moment, your readers expect you to take a stand. Nobody wants the media to be calm and objective any more. Citizens are scarcely able to demonstrate any more, there are no functioning associations to take their part, freedoms are increasingly restricted, so if there is a newspaper that says Erdogan must go, that is what you want.'

So that is what he does, and he continues: 'The government has deprived us of our objectivity. That is the point where the political conflict starts. As an editor and as a journalist you have to be brave to stick to it, or rich, ready for a fight or ready to be locked up in prison.'

Asked whether Cumhuriyet will still exist in six months' time or could possibly be banned, Can Dündar shrugs his shoulders. 'There will probably be fresh elections, and a lot will depend on them,' he says. 'Will the AKP be in power on its own again, or will they still have to look seriously for a coalition partner?'

Suddenly he gets up to turn up the TV's sound. Prime Minister Davutoglu is giving a press conference to say that the coalition negotiations have finally broken down. There will be fresh elections that are later set down for 1 November 2015. The interview is over, as he has to go back to work. Dündar's secretary takes a photograph of him and the writer, who is herself under surveillance for 'making propaganda for a terrorist organisation' and who later posts the photograph on Twitter. Over the following days various pro-government newspapers pick up the photograph, adding inflammatory, offensive captions on 'spies', 'terrorists' and 'provocation'. That is how things are.

_ Terrorists, spies and traitors

There was widespread condemnation directed at the Turkish government when the well known journalist and editor of the independent newspaper Cumhuriyet, Can Dündar, and the head of Cumhuriyet's Ankara bureau, Erdem Gül, were detained at the end of November 2015 and taken a few days later to the prison in Silivri, to the west of Istanbul. Fifteen Turkish and international press organisations demanded the two be released immediately. The European Commission termed the arrests 'disturbing' and made clear it was closely following developments in Turkey. Newspapers all over the world wrote about the case and published editorials on press freedom. Twitter and Facebook exploded with indignation and rage.

It needs to be said out loud, because keeping silent is not an option, but of course it makes no difference. According to the Turkish government, the issue with Dündar and Gül is not one of journalism, but of terrorism, espionage and treason. When Erdogan threatened immediately following Cumhuriyet's scoop that those publishing the story would pay a high price, he also mentioned the word 'spies'. So if you count the journalists in Turkish prisons, then for President Erdogan, Dündar and Gül do not count.

If you count the journalists in captivity, then according to the AKP government's criteria, you end up with zero in any case. At the end of December 2015 Justice Minister Bekir Bozdag said in response to questions on detained journalists: 'At the moment there are journalists in prison in Turkey. But if you look at the charges laid against those remanded in custody, it turns out that they are not being prosecuted on account of their work as journalists. The convicted journalists too have not been convicted on account of their work. The crimes attributed to them are of another order. No single journalist is being prosecuted in Turkey for their work. In the case of the persons you referred to as well, there are other charges laid.' The latter was aimed at Can Dündar and Erdem Gül, about whom one journalist asked a specific question.

For example, the journalist who has been in prison longest, Hatice Duman, was convicted of 'activities against the state', in other words: terrorism. The fact that she never picked up a weapon, but was only editor of the magazine Atilim (Leap) up until her imprisonment in 2003, is not a factor in the Turkish political and legal system.

The same applies to Seyithan Akyüz, a reporter at the Kurdish language newspaper Azadiya Welat, who was locked up for the same offence in 2009. Mehmet Baransu, a journalist for the newspaper Taraf and co-responsible for reporting on ultimately unproven plans to mount a coup against the AKP government, is in jail for 'setting up a criminal organisation' and 'acquiring, publishing and destroying documents related to the security of the state'.

According to the letter of the law, Justice Minister Bozdag may be right, but it is precisely the laws that are the problem. The law on terrorism, often used against journalists, is so vague that any activity could fall under it, including writing a piece. So, whatever international journalist associations, human rights organisations and EU politicians might say, Turkey reacts or declines to do so, or says that no journalists are involved, but rather common criminals or terrorists. So then what's left to discuss?

The same applies to the hundreds of legal cases against the media and journalists. Perhaps even thousands – no one knows precisely how many there are, as it is simply impossible to keep track. Lawyers working for the independent newspapers Taraf and Cumhuriyet have their work cut out dealing with all the legal cases properly, launching appeals against convictions in time, appearing in court to defend their clients against one absurd charge after another.

Apart from newspapers, individual journalists are charged as well. And once the public prosecutor has you in his sights, whether or not at the behest of President Erdogan, it normally does not stop at one case: there are journalists who do not even know how many cases are currently pending against them and who simply shrug their shoulders in utter impotence.

Many of the cases lead to suspended sentences. Engage in propaganda for a terrorist organisation just once more, comment on a case currently before the courts once more, publish secret documents once more, and you go to prison or have to pay a large fine. The classic way of course of forcing journalists to censor themselves.

_ The AKP's mouthpiece
But prosecuting and locking up journalists costs time and money and also draws attention, and so the government has increasingly resorted to having reporters and particularly columnists fired. At the end of 2014, the CHP opposition party brought out a voluminous report on this entitled 'Journalists whose pen has been broken' ('Kalemi kiralan gazeteciler' in

Turkish). The CHP estimated that, in the 12 years that the AKP had then been in power, as many as 1,863 journalists had been fired or forced to resign for political reasons.

The peak occurred around the Gezi protests that erupted in Istanbul, Ankara and other cities in the spring of 2013, initially against the demolition of Gezi, a small park in the heart of Istanbul, but by degrees against the increasingly authoritarian policies of Erdogan, prime minister at the time: in the two months following the start of the protests at the end of May 2013, 22 journalists were fired and 37 forced to resign, according to figures from Turkey's journalists' trade union, the TGS.

Dismissals of this order do not go unnoticed, but the international community worries about them much less. International journalists' organizations focus primarily on journalists who have been imprisoned, and for human rights organizations journalists who have been fired often do not fall within their mandate at all. The EU does not get excited about dismissals, and the international media devote at best a small report on their inside pages to dismissed fellow journalists whom hardly anyone outside Turkey knows.

Something that has also not been as extreme as it is now is the number of newspapers falling directly under the government's control. The most striking example is the daily Sabah, effectively the AKP's mouthpiece. This newspaper was established in 1985 and was long seen as quality-wise not bad, but it was taken over by the government in 2007, officially because the regulations had not been adhered to during a previous takeover in 2001. Ownership of Sabah was passed to a company of which Erdogan's son-in-law, Berat Albayrak, was a director. In 2013 Sabah was bought by the Kalyon Group, a company big in project development and construction that has close links to the AKP government. So close, that it was awarded the contract for the construction of Istanbul's third airport and made large profits from constructing Istanbul's metrobus system.

Sabah has for long not been anything like a 'newspaper'. For the Kalyon Group, Sabah is merely an instrument for currying favour with the government and the president as far as possible and securing large construction contracts as a result.

And Sabah is not the only one. There is now an entire series of newspapers, all in the hands of major companies that are also engaged in construction, telecoms, industry and infrastructure, cosying up to the government too closely to be able to earn the hallmark 'journalism'. Frequently they all carry precisely the same lurid front page headline in the morning, either setting the government in a good light or maligning the opposition.

Are there still journalists in Turkey, and independent newspapers? Yes, there are. But their scope of action is diminishing by the day. The pressure on those taking their calling seriously is huge: dismissal, prosecution or being imprisoned hang like a sword of Damocles over their heads every day.

At the beginning of December 2015, Bülent Kenes, the editor of Today's Zaman, the English edition of the Turkish daily Zaman, resigned because in his own words he was no longer able to work under all the pressure that was being applied to him and his newspaper. He had been editor since the newspaper was set up in January 2007. On resigning he said: 'I tried my hardest to do my work to the best of my ability, in order to maintain the newspaper's integrity and to resist all the pressure from the government as far as possible.' He continues to work for the newspaper as a columnist.

Kenes gave up after receiving a suspended 21 month jail sentence on being convicted of defaming President Erdogan on Twitter (in 14 tweets that did not so much as contain the president's name) and facing a whole series of cases initiated by Erdogan, Prime Minister Davutoglu and other government members, and after he had been detained between 10 and 14 October. All the cases concerned his work as a journalist.

Without detracting in any way from Kenes' personal decision to call it a day, many journalists refuse to allow themselves to be intimidated. This emerged for instance from the words of Vildan Atmaca, a reporter for the Jinha news agency, which focuses its reporting primarily on Kurdish women. On release in December 2015 after being remanded in custody for 46 days, she said: 'I do not feel intimidated by what I have been through, and I will continue to describe the violations of rights and other problems that people experience.' She was detained along with a colleague in the eastern province of Van and accused of 'propaganda for a terrorist organisation' and of 'defaming President Erdogan'.

_ Outside the lines drawn by the state

If Turkey remains totally deaf to criticism of the increasing lack of press freedom and, all things considered, the freedom of the press is restricted more every day, what would make a real difference in changing the situation for the better?

Would it help if President Erdogan disappeared from the scene? After all, he is the one who imposes his will on the legal system, he is the one who determines which journalists are fired, detained or maligned, behind the scenes and sometimes out in the open, he is the one who has an increasing number of newspapers and TV channels in his iron grip. Conditions have never been as dire for the freedom of the press in Turkey as they are now.

The statistics show this too, by the way. In the Press Freedom Index of Freedom House Turkey has been listed as 'not free' since 2013, dropping from 'partly free' in the three years prior to that. In the Press Freedom Index from Reporters Without Borders, Turkey has dropped steadily from place 100 (of 180) in 2002 (the first year the Index was published) to place 149 in 2015.

Nevertheless, simply to state that the end of Erdogan's dominance will set the press free would bypass the deeper truths of the media landscape and Turkish law. Erdogan may have propelled the suppression of free journalism to an unheard of level, but to do this he is making use of existing systems, the existing dynamics in the media, the existing legal system and the existing constitution.

Irrespective of the government that was in power before the AKP, the press has not been free in the past. Dozens of journalists were murdered in the 1990s, for decades the army had the main say in reporting on state matters in the broadest sense of the term, newspapers and TV channels have never had the chance to operate outside the lines drawn by the state.

There is no reason to believe that things will be different if the AKP government were to vacate the field in favour of a government under the leadership of the parties now in opposition. On the contrary, polarisation in Turkey has reached such a pitch that rejection, and even hatred, of the AKP and Erdogan is now so intense that it could be pay-back time once one of the established opposition parties takes over the reins. Who will guarantee that those now using their pens or cameras to defend Erdogan through thick and thin will not be detained in their turn and locked up for 'supporting a coup', for 'supporting terrorism' or for 'membership of a criminal organisation'? No one.

The laws, and above all the mentality, that make it possible to muzzle journalists lie deeply entrenched in the Turkish political system. Just as the AKP is, and just as the old and established political parties, the CHP (the largest opposition party, the Republican People's Party) and the MHP (the ultra-nationalist Nationalist Action Party) are. The AKP, the CHP and the MHP are similar to each other. They are established on the principles of the republic as it was founded in 1923, including the indivisible unity of the state, including the fundamental principle that every Turkish citizen is a Turk, including the deeply rooted fear that the outside world and the enemies within are always out to weaken and divide Turkey. The laws that the AKP is currently using against journalists are part of that system and of that package of values. Any party that does away with these laws is basically undermining the foundations of the state. Inconceivable. And the use, more precisely the misuse, of these political laws for political advantage? Too tempting, too effective not to be used. Too accepted by Turkish society as well.

For that reason, the underlying dynamic will have to be tackled in order for the press to be truly free. The dynamic of the ownership of media concerns, that of the legal framework in which Turkish journalism has to operate, and even the foundations of the Republic of Turkey as presently constituted.

HRANT DINK (1954-2007)

The journalist and intellectual Hrant Dink was the voice of the Armenian community in Turkey. He was the editor of Agos, a bilingual newspaper that he had set up himself, when he was shot down in broad daylight on the pavement in front of the Agos offices. The perpetrator was a nationalist who was still a minor.

Dink worked by means of his newspaper and in interviews, speeches and lectures to achieve reconciliation between Turks and Armenians – a relationship that has been troubled since the Armenian genocide at the beginning of the 20th century. In his work he called for complete freedom of expression, as in his view reconciliation could be achieved only through dialogue. He also opposed laws, for instance in France, that made denial of the Armenian genocide punishable. Through his work he initiated a discussion within the Armenian community, both in Turkey and in the diaspora, about how best to deal with the past.

Dink increasingly came under fire for his work in Turkey. He was regarded as a 'traitor' by Turkish nationalists. A nationalist lawyer initiated legal action against Dink in response to a column in Agos. In the column Dink called on Armenians to distance themselves 'from the Turkish component of their blood' and to orient themselves towards their new fatherland – Armenia. By this he meant that the anger that many Armenians feel towards Turkey on account of the events of 1915 was harming primarily the Armenians themselves and that they should rather look to the future. In the nationalist lawyer's view the column was an affront to 'Turkishness', which was forbidden in terms of Article 301 of the criminal code.

Initially Dink was not particularly concerned about the charge, saying that he had confidence in the law. His confidence was not borne out: he received a six-month suspended sentence, confirmed on appeal. The trial drew a great deal of attention, with the result that Dink was repeatedly linked in the media to allegations of insulting the Turkish national identity. Threats from extremist Turkish nationalists ensued. During the months before his death Dink felt constantly on his guard, like a pigeon looking over his shoulder in fear, as he wrote in his last Agos column. His assailant, Ogun Samast, a 17-year-old youth from the Black Sea port of Trabzon, which has a nationalist reputation, was soon picked up. In 2011 he was convicted under the juvenile code and sentenced to 22 years and 10 months in jail. At the trial he pleaded not guilty to murder, blaming the newspapers that termed Dink a 'traitor' in their headlines.

The fact that the murderer is in jail does not mean that the Hrant Dink case has been finally solved. The investigation showed clearly that there were many within the police hierarchy in both Trabzon and Istanbul who were well aware of the threats made on Dink and of the concrete plans to murder him. The Dink family lawyers and his widow Rakel have ever since been doing their utmost to have all of those responsible brought to justice. The task seems impossible at present: those responsible are protecting each other right up to senior level. Numerous investigations and cases are currently underway to reveal the truth.

Apart from his wife Rakel, Hrant Dink left three adult children: Arat, Delal and Sera.

CHAPTER 2

OWNERSHIP

There is an anecdote about chicken. It takes place in a small town somewhere in Turkey – the story does not make clear where precisely – where the local newspaper was owned by a businessman who also dealt in chicken. Every day the newspaper printed an item on the delights, versatility and health benefits of this white meat. Until the newspaper changed owners. Chicken disappeared from the pages.

That is what determines Turkey's media landscape and journalism, although on a huge scale. In print and also on TV, still the two main ways in Turkey of keeping up with the news.

Commercialisation of the Turkish media began in the 1980s, when Prime Minister Turgut Özal embarked on far-reaching liberalisation of the Turkish economy. The media had previously been allied to political parties, and there was the TRT state broadcaster. Commercialisation initiated the current era: the first players that were not originally from the world of the media and journalism entered the news market.

Large companies saw potential. Strategic use of newspapers and TV broadcasters allowed them to contribute to company profits. One business corporation after another began to publish newspapers with the intention of using them strategically. Often several newspapers in order to reach different target groups. Mass-circulation newspapers with hardly any text and a great many (celebrity) pictures, newspapers for the middle class who tend slightly to the left or alternatively to the right, newspapers for religious conservatives, newspapers for football fans. During the course of the 1990s, an increasing number of commercial TV channels came onto the market, and from the second half of the 1990s, broadcasters putting out 24-hour news.

The idea that a media landscape determined by commercial interests is least vulnerable to censorship and other state influence is often part of global thinking on the freedom of the media. After all, party political interests then have less influence.

A glance at large international media organizations is perhaps of interest in that light. Consider CNN of the US, the first TV channel to focus on news 24 hours a day, established in 1980. It is owned by Turner Broadcasting System, a division of Time Warner, a media multinational that focuses solely on the media. Or the BBC in the UK: a public corporation financed with public money. The New York Times is published by the New York Times Company, with no interests outside journalism. The Wall Street Journal, the largest US newspaper, is owned by Dow Jones & Company, which is in turn part of News Corp, like Time Warner a media multinational. The world's largest newspaper, Japan's Yomiuri Shimbun, is owned by the Shimbun Group, Japan's largest media concern. The UK's Guardian? Part of the Guardian Media Group, which is part of The Scott Trust Limited, a trust fund established to ensure the newspaper's journalistic independence.

Of course this does not mean that these media are beacons in the stormy seas of the media, where choices are made every day again purely on journalistic criteria. An increasing number of media companies are listed on the stock exchange and so have shareholders to keep happy. This applies to Time Warner and News Corp, and also for example to British newspapers like the Sunday Times and the Independent, and the Dutch NRC, Volkskrant and Telegraaf. This puts journalistic choices under pressure and makes it more difficult to print stories on subjects that address a smaller group of readers, not to mention stories that could offend the companies that buy the adverts that keep these media alive. But in Turkey the relationship is different. A commercial market can make the media (more) free and independent of censorship and influence from the state, but only under condition that the state withdraws from the economy. In many countries high on the lists of press freedom put out by the international monitoring organisations, this is indeed the case.

However, in Turkey the state is still a major player in the economy and is certainly not about to withdraw from an economic role. The state, and thus the government, have a firm grip on the economy and are in a position to make or break companies.

What does this mean in practice? That companies that have media divisions must keep the government on their side, certainly if it is a one-party government like that run by the AKP for almost 14 years now. Example. The construction sector has increasingly been the motor driving the Turkish economy, with huge sums of money being turned over. The state acts as facilitator, not only by making sites available and issuing permits, but is also active itself in the market. Over recent decades, so-called TOKI complexes have been built in virtually every Turkish city. These are huge accommodation blocks on the outskirts providing apartments for sale to people on a middle income at advantageous rates funded by the state. TOKI is a state project. A company wishing to be involved in the development or construction of them, whether as building contractor, road builder or supplier of doors or windows, will be compelled to maintain good relations with the state (i.e. the government). If you as a company can deploy your newspapers and TV stations to make the state more favourably disposed towards you then you do not pass up this opportunity.

One of the most striking examples of the mingling of media and construction sector interests was mentioned in the last chapter, namely the Kalyon Group, owner of the government's mouthpiece newspaper Sabah. Its construction division is currently building Istanbul's third airport. And there is a connection with the 2013 Gezi protests: the protests were initially directed purely at the disappearance of Gezi Park, an island of green in the city that was to have given way to a project in which an army barracks that once stood there could be rebuilt to serve as a shopping centre. The project's developer? Correct: Kalyon.

Once the demonstrations spilled over into a broader protest against the ever more authoritarian Erdogan government, Sabah was one of the dailies that used every column to denigrate the protests as violent and to depict the demonstrators as ruffians, terrorists, looters, atheists (a synonym in Turkey for those without morals), traitors and pawns in a global plot to undermine Turkey motivated by unadulterated jealousy of its rising strength.

The debate in Turkey is virtually never about the readership and audience numbers of newspapers and TV stations, about how to halt the decline in newspaper readership, about experimenting with new business models to keep the media going in a digitalising world. This is partly to do with this dynamic between the media, business life and the state. Newspapers and TV stations are not there for journalistic reasons and not even in the first instance to turn a profit on their own, and they are not shut down, sold or merged with other providers if they are in need of too much money. They are an investment, part of the business strategy, and they are permitted to cost quite a bit of money, as long as they do their work effectively as marketing, propaganda and networking tools.

_ Auditing the books

In 2009 the head of one of Turkey's largest business empires, the media tycoon Aydin Dogan, found out what not toeing the line can cost. His newspapers, a broad spectrum at the time including well known names like Hürriyet, Posta, Milliyet, Vatan, Radikal, (a sports sheet) Fanatik and CNNTürk, had dared to voice increasing criticism of the AKP government, after having supported it in the initial years it was in government after 2001.

Things went awry in September 2009, when the Dogan publishing group was hit with a huge tax fine. Analysts and observers immediately came to the conclusion that the fine was punishment by the government for reports on alleged AKP corruption, among other things. Erdogan spoke out repeatedly against the media group in public, calling on AKP members and indirectly the Turkish population not to buy Dogan newspapers any more. The tax fine was a record at 2.5 billion dollars, as much as four fifths of the combined market value of the Dogan Media Group and parent company Dogan Holding.

Prime Minister Erdogan vehemently denied that the fine was politically motivated, but no one believed him. Tax fines are one of the ways in which the Turkish government deals with wealthy opponents. For example, no one was amazed at the audit of the books at Koc Holding, one of Turkey's largest companies in the summer of 2013. Koc is owner of the Divan Hotel next to Gezi Park in Istanbul, where the major protest movement against the AKP government began at the end of May 2013. The protest movement was vigorously put down by the police, and demonstrators fled the tear gas and water cannon to seek shelter in the Divan Hotel. Erdogan expressed his displeasure at this in clear terms when in a speech he accused the hotel of being an accessory to crime. Suddenly in July tax office auditors were at the front doors of various branches of Koc Holding all over the country, accompanied by the police.

This was normal procedure, according to government representatives, including Energy Minister Taner Yildiz, who said a day after the operation: 'Audits of the books are routine for the Finance Ministry.' The independent daily Taraf investigated the history of similar combined tax office and police operations and came to the conclusion that this was by no means routine. Operations of this kind had until then only been used against companies suspected of being involved in drug dealing or terrorism, or large scale fraud.

But what can you do if you as (media) concern are hit with a politically motivated tax operation like this? Attempting to resist, for instance through the courts, is a complete waste of time. As Cumhuriyet editor Can Dündar said in the interview in Chapter 1, the AKP rules on its own and makes maximum use of the holes in the system that allow it to bring under its control an increasing number of state institutions that should operate independently. No internal appeal procedure at the tax office will come down on Dogan's side if the battle is with Erdogan. No judge will hand down a verdict in favour of an opponent of the president or the governing party.

It is not just a few newspapers that are completely dependent on the government in this way; they nearly all are, although there are differences in degree. A number of newspapers are direct spokespersons for the AKP government and write precisely what the government wants. These include Türkiye, Sabah (Morning), Aksam (Evening), Star, Yeni Safak (New Dawn) and Yeni Akit (New Contract), and TV stations like AHaber and ATV. State TV TRT and the official Anadolu news agency have become nothing more than government mouthpieces. As an example: Erdogan's press adviser, Kemal Öztürk, was appointed in 2011 to the most senior position at Anadolu, from which he resigned in 2015 to seek a seat in parliament for the AKP. On failing to do so, he became a columnist at Yeni Safak, or as the newspaper put it, 'he became a member of the Yeni Safak family'.
The intensity of the entanglement emerged when Hasan Karakaya, the editor of Yeni Akit, the newspaper known as the most inflammatory, mendacious and anti-Semitic in Turkey, died when he was visiting Saudi Arabia as part of President Erdogan's entourage in December 2015. The official visit was broken off for Erdogan and various other government representatives to attend the man's funeral. Everyone praised Karakaya's sharp pen.

The examples of newspapers that print precisely the same headlines on the front page are striking. On 7 June 2013 Zaman, Star, Yeni Safak, Sabah, HaberTürk, Bugün and Türkiye all headed their front pages with: Demokratik talebe canim feda, or 'Democratic demands are welcome', a quote from a speech made by Erdogan following a visit to three North African countries while the Arab Spring was underway and Erdogan was having to deal with the Gezi protests at home. Erdogan was shown as a man who wanted to listen to reasonable demands for democracy, while depicting the Gezi demonstrators as troublemakers. On May 2015, a week before the general elections, as many as five newspapers headlined: 'Ihanetin ilaci yok', or 'There is no medicine against treason'. The accompanying story was about Cumhuriyet's scoop, published the day before regarding MIT weapons transports to Syria, to the effect that – according to Erdogan – the transports were medicines, not weapons. Cumhuriyet and its editor Can Dündar were dismissed as traitors. The video film showing the search of the trucks was reported to have been leaked to Cumhuriyet by people within the state apparatus linked to Fethullah Gülen, the Turkish Muslim cleric living in the US. His movement, which once worked closely with the AKP, was said to be aiming to topple the government, intending to plot a 'coup' and were thus 'terrorists' on that basis.

Of course, none of the government newspapers printed a serious news item on Cumhuriyet's scoop or devoted a story to what had in fact come to light regarding the transports.

On 5 March 2015 this headline trend reached a new low: on that day 14 columns in five different newspapers bore the same headline: 'Diliniz kaba, vicdaniniz tas', or 'Your language is shameless, your conscience is hard as stone'. The headline could be seen as many as five times in a single edition of Yeni Safak and Star.

It all concerned an incident reported to have taken place during the 2013 Gezi protests that had been widely reported in the government media. In that incident a woman wearing a headscarf and pushing a stroller with a toddler in it was said to have been assaulted by a group of men clad in leather. The story turned out to be false, as was later acknowledged by those publishing the 'scoop', and security camera footage showed the woman concerned simply walking by without a hair on her head being touched.

The incident was heavily exploited to discredit the Gezi demonstrators who were accused of being behind it. The now notorious 'Kabatas incident', named after the Istanbul district where it did not take place, was raked up again at the start of 2015, with the 14 columnists deciding to take sides on behalf of the liars and of women wearing headscarves. The wordplay, with kaba (shameless) and tas (stone) forming

Kabatas, made the subject of the column clear to everyone. Significantly this took place three months before parliamentary elections – many AKP voters had heard of the incident that never happened and were not at all convinced that it was a lie. The fact that 14 pro-government columnists took up pens again on behalf of women wearing headscarves suited the AKP's religious following.

_ At first sight reasonable journalism

Apart from the newspapers and TV channels acting as mouthpieces for the AKP, there are dailies and broadcasters offering support to the government in a less obvious way. These are frequently large newspapers seen as mainstream, including Milliyet, HaberTürk and Hürriyet. From them no blaring pro-Erdogan slogans on the front page or as the first items in news programmes, no unscrupulous attacks on every Erdogan opponent, rather reasonable journalism with non-inflammatory headlines at first sight. And that is frequently the case, except that these newspapers' true allegiance emerges from the contributions of their columnists. Every newspaper has a string of them, and they are generally well remunerated for their service, as well as being highly respected (by contrast on both counts with the reporters getting their boots dirty trying to gather the news every day). Close analysis of the columns shows that over recent years there has scarcely been any criticism of the government. Any columnist daring to do so, or taking up subject matters seen as taboo, can be paid off at a moment's notice. In the major newspapers there are hardly any columnists prepared to voice strong criticism of Erdogan or of government policy anymore. The columnists remaining have toned down their articles, while those refusing to do so have been put out on the street.

An outstanding example is the well known columnist Bekir Coskun, who for years had a permanent corner in one of Turkey's largest newspapers, Hürriyet, from the Dogan stable. Coskun was fired on 9 September 2009, just one day after the tax authorities had imposed the astronomic fine of 2.5 billion dollars on the Dogan Media Group. Coskun moved to HaberTürk, which he left a year later after an argument, to go over to the independent Cumhuriyet. He has now left there as well, his columns appearing in Sözcü since 2013.

According to the leader of the largest opposition party CHP, Kemal Kilicdaroglu, Coskun's departure from HaberTürk had to do with a business deal. HaberTürk's parent company, the Ciner Group, was said to be involved in tendering for the construction of a power station. Firing Bekir Coskun, a staunch secularist and Erdogan opponent whose pieces were increasingly sharp in their criticism, was said to be part of the deal. True? Not true? No Turkish newspaper was prepared probe to the bottom of this.

Amberin Zaman, Turkey correspondent for The Economist from 1999 to 2015, a journalist of long standing for various Turkish and international media and currently reporter and columnist for the independent Turkish online news platform Diken (Thorn) and a fellow at the Woodrow Wilson Center in Washington DC, has experienced restrictions on press freedom in many ways. She recalls a visit by then Prime Minister Erdogan to Qatar in January 2013. At the time she was working for The Economist and the daily HaberTürk, two major publications, which ensured a place on board the official aircraft.

'My problems began to get serious when I continued to write critically about the government following the trip,' Zaman said in an interview conducted on Skype in February 2016. 'I was being constantly spoken to about my columns by my boss at the newspaper. I was told to be careful about what I wrote. I knew then that the question was not so much whether but when I would bedismissed. One evening as I was having dinner with a friend, my editor rang and asked, laughing nervously, whether I remembered the topic we had discussed previously. I immediately understood and asked whether he meant that I had been fired. He said yes.'

It was the beginning of April 2013. Zaman went to Taraf, a newspaper known for not paying its columnists. Taraf columnists can

do little about this, because they are often journalists that have been pushed out elsewhere on account of voicing critical opinions and are having difficulty finding a new paid position. If you are fired from a major publication, you won't be able to find a place at other newspapers that do pay but are also economically dependent on
the government. It was a financial blow for Zaman, but she still had The Economist and soon began working for the Washington-based online news portal Al-Monitor, and she could always express her opinions through Taraf.

Has she ever considered writing with greater caution for fear of censorship or government pressures ? Not for a moment, she says. 'I'm not a criminal. I've done nothing wrong, and editors do not need a reason to dismiss you, because it is all pure politics. Look at the Baransu case (see Chapter 3) and other cases. That is what can happen to you if you transgress the limits of what the government sees as good journalism.' What is also interesting is that Zaman believes that in the years 2002 to around 2010 she was freer than ever as a journalist. She says: 'Erdogan had just come to power, and Turkey became more democratic, freer. That began to change around 2010. Erdogan grew overconfident, partly because he had cut back the military's power and had amended the constitution (giving the government more power over the legal system, FG) and also because of the lack of a credible opposition. It went downhill after that.'

Previously Zaman often worked in the south-east of the country, for the Los Angeles Times and the Washington Post. 'I wrote a lot about Kurds and was for example in Cizre during Newroz in 1992[1]. The authorities hated what I wrote. One day there was an article about me on the front page of a newspaper under the headline 'This is the woman causing problems', alongside a photograph that they had obviously obtained from the Information Ministry. A TV programme added its little bit. Suddenly there were journalists camped outside my house clamouring to talk to me, photograph me so that I couldn't go out the door any more. I didn't know what to do, and even considered stopping work as a journalist.'

1 See biography of murdered journalist Izzet Kezer on page 112

She relates how she was on occasion detained by the police in the south-east during those years. Nevertheless that did not feel as threatening as the situation now, she says looking back. 'The pressure is now coming from all sides, and the animosity directed at me is so personal. That makes it more difficult to carry on with reporting.'

Concretely that means for instance that government representatives no longer talk to her, whereas Prime Minister Davutoglu for example used to do so up to the June 2015 elections. She has access only to anonymous sources within the AKP, who are for journalistic reasons more problematic to use in articles. There was in addition a threat from ISIS, with the result that for months she did not feel it was safe for her to travel to the border zone with Syria, even though there was great news interest. To cap it all, it turned out that the MIT, the Turkish intelligence service, had tapped her phone in 2008 and 2009, like those of many fellow journalists, and she was suddenly named in a case related to terrorism and a coup.

In 2014, Erdogan pilloried Zaman in public. Zaman drew his anger during a CNNTürk programme, in which the leader of the largest opposition party the CHP, Kemal Kilicdaroglu, was a guest to be interviewed by a number of journalists, including Zaman. Kilicdaroglu expressed his concern over the fact that people unquestioningly embraced Erdogan. Zaman responded that critical thought was discouraged by Turkey's national education system and that in a country where Islamic tarikats (brotherhoods) had so much influence and promoted consensus versus individualism it may be unrealistic to expect critical thinking.

The issue erupted on Twitter on a whole barrage of accounts that are often described as the AKP Twitter army. Zaman and Kilicdaroglu were labelled 'enemies of Islam'. Things deteriorated when Erdogan not much later called Zaman a 'shameless militant disguised as a journalist' during a meeting, without mentioning her name, but referring to the programme with the opposition leader. 'You insult a society that is 99% Muslim. Know your place!', he added.

A hate campaign of unheard of dimensions was generated on Twitter – which ironically iillustrated the phenomenon about which Kilicdaroglu and Zaman had exchanged ideas live on TV. Amberin Zaman: 'I responded to Erdogan in my column. Then things got worse. He attacked me during another campaign rally for a second day running. He referred to me as 'scum'. Again, he didn't name me but it was obvious to everyone who he was talking about. I was inundated with death and rape threats.' For a long time, she did not feel safe on the street, going about her work, fearful of being recognised and attacked. She has faced judicial investigation in three separate criminal complaints launched against here, including one by Erdogan.

But stop being a journalist? Zaman: 'No, all of this reinforced my conviction that this what I need to do.' The fact that she has been living in Washington DC since August 2015 has partly to do with the attacks on her, but certainly not everything. The reasons are primarily private – she is married to a US diplomat who was posted to Washington. Zaman returns to Turkey regularly for reporting trips. 'I always get my lawyer to check whether there are fresh cases pending against me before I retun.' She adds: 'But I think it's nice to be in Washington now. It is good observe everything from a distance for a change.'

_ Terrorism and incidents of violence

CNNTürk still from time to time has the courage to invite guests onto live talk shows that are not in the government's camp, but at these huge broadcasters, including NTV, you can see that they are subservient to Erdogan not only by those they invite, but more importantly by those they do not invite.

In the summer of 2011 the head of NTV vehemently denied that the dismissal of the well known talk show hostess Banu Güven had anything to do with pressure from Ankara and insisted that there was simply no new programme available for her in the new season. That did not sound in the least convincing, if only because Güven was the broadcaster's most popular anchor and always recorded outstanding viewing figures – crucial to a commercial broadcaster.

The truth was probably that Güven, who had been working for NTV for 14 years, gave her bosses an increasingly uncomfortable feeling with her show, in which she asked penetrating questions of a single guest. The guests and the topics became increasingly controversial, and subjects like the Kurdish question are extremely sensitive, certainly if they are broadcast live, as with Güven. Before NTV fired her, screenwriter, poet and novelist Vedat Türkali for instance was a guest. He expressed open support for the imprisoned leader of the armed Kurdish PKK. Güven's suggestion to her bosses to invite Leyla Zana, a famous Kurdish human rights activist and politician, was rejected. Soon afterwards Güven disappeared from the screen. The Türkali broadcast was removed from the NTV online archives. In a statement put out by NTV after Güven's dismissal, NTV director Cem Aydin said that the broadcaster 'had never had requests from the government or any political party whatever to work with particular persons'. And that could well be true. The Turkish media of their own accord know roughly where the borders lie. It is evident that border has been completely transgressed when something positive is said about Abdullah Öcalan during a popular live programme, and that those allowing this to happen will have to accept the consequences. No phone call from Ankara needed.

Aydin's denial that the AKP government had ever made 'requests' regarding working or not working with particular people came to be seen in a different light three months later. In October 2011 both Ferit Şahenk, the head of the board of management of Dogus Holding (owner of NTV) and Nermin Yurteri, NTV editor in chief, were present at a meeting where the elite of the Turkish media world received instructions from Erdogan in person on what to publish and broadcast. Media tycoon and founder of the Dogan business empire Aydin Dogan was also there to pay his respects, despite having had a huge tax fine imposed in 2009 for disloyalty to the government.

Following the press gathering with Prime Minister Erdogan various news agencies, including the semi-official Anadolu, which is used by virtually all the media, stated that they would obey the publication bans imposed by the authorities. When reporting news concerning 'terrorism and incidents of violence' they would 'take public order into account', they said. In addition they promised to 'distance themselves from reporting that might give rise to fear, chaos, animosity, panic and intimidation' and that 'no publication at all will contain propaganda for an illegal organisation'. NTV fell into line as well. CNNTürk, Milliyet, Hürriyet, HaberTürk all agreed. Yasemin Congar, deputy editor of the independent daily Taraf, a newspaper that was campaigning strongly against the army at the time, wrote a day after the gathering with Erdogan, which she also attended, that she found it breath-taking to see how media bosses made more proposals than Erdogan himself to 'standardise' the press.

In an interview in Istanbul one and a half years after the meeting, Congar said: 'It started with a speech by Erdogan. In it he discussed what he described as the thin dividing line between propaganda and journalism. The rest of the meeting was closed and 'off the record', but I am now able to speak about it. Aydin Dogan suggested setting up a group of publishers and editors to draw up rules on how sensitive news should be published. Government representatives should also sit on the group, he said, but Erdogan said that was not necessary. I don't know whether the group ever met. Another proposed three main rules: not inviting people who do not term the PKK a terrorist organisation, not talking to the PKK or visiting their camps on the border with Iraq, because that constitutes propaganda for the PKK, and limiting to 15 seconds breaking news on violence linked to the struggle against the PKK.'

There was also discussion on halting visits to 'certain places' and talking to 'certain people', Congar says. Congar: 'Because no one said anything about it, I have at last opened my mouth and said that I was one of the people that visited 'certain places' and spoke to 'certain people' and that I would certainly continue to do so.' Congar was subsequently complimented on her protest by fellow editors: 'But during the meeting everyone kept their mouths shut, frightened of the publishers and owners of their newspaper who were also present. Taraf's owner was also there, but Taraf is independent and not part of a large company, so I have greater freedom.'[2]

In addition the discussion altered nothing in existing practice, but merely reconfirmed the unwritten rules, and the audience with Erdogan added extra weight.

The timing of the meeting was also interesting: it was two days after a major attack by the PKK in Hakkari Province, in which 24 soldiers were killed and 22 injured. The prime minister was possibly not entirely satisfied with the reporting by many newspapers and broadcasters, although they adhered closely to the conventions: heightened emotion, yet more nationalism, a great deal of war and vengeance rhetoric, showing the flag without let-up and endless repeats of the most heart-rending images. Erdogan possibly also knew that the government's vengeance would be sweet, and the idea was to instruct the press in a timely and proper manner.

The big test came on 28 December 2011. That evening the Turkish army aimed to deliver a heavy blow to the PKK with an airstrike on a group of people crossing the border between Iraq and Turkey, high in the snow-covered mountains. But it quickly emerged that the group bombed was not a PKK unit, but a group of Kurdish civilians smuggling petrol, cigarettes and tea. A long-established way for people in the region to make a living, certainly since the armed struggle between the PKK and the army broke out in 1984, which meant that other work in the border zone, such as animal husbandry, was no longer available. As many as 34 people, including 19 minors, were killed in the bombing.

Kurdish media, which take little notice of orders from the Turkish authorities, were soon at the scene and reported the news to the world, including photographs of the bodies being carried down from the mountains on mules. However, the Turkish media did not pick up the story at all. The next morning, some 10 hours after the bombing, the major

2 Interview with Yasemin Congar previously published in 'The Boys are Dead', Fréderike Geerdink, Gomidas Books, 2015.

news broadcasters and the newspapers were still silent on the 34 dead Turkish citizens. Not even the news tickers at the bottom of the screen said anything about what had happened. A presenter from one of the major news broadcasters revealed anonymously through Twitter that there had been phone calls from Ankara immediately after the incident banning the media from reporting on the deaths until the story had been confirmed by officials.

That confirmation came at noon, more than 12 hours after the bombs had been dropped, in the shape of an army press statement. TV broadcasters were summoned to broadcast it, and they did. The statement was devoid of content. The attack was described as an incident in the battle against terrorism, and that was the end of the matter.

It is important to note here that Turkey's newspapers are not full of lies and incitement from front to back. There is sound reporting, there are good news stories, there are scoops, good journalists and columnists, and if you keep track of a number of different media, you are reasonably well informed on what is going on in the country. The sad thing is that this is so despite the system. Despite the ownership, despite the virtually endless series of court cases against journalists, newspapers and TV stations, despite the threat of dismissal that hangs over the heads of journalists and columnists every day. The pressure increases by the day, and given that the courage has to come from individual journalists and that the system works against them, publishing the news is increasingly restricted.

HAFIZ AKDEMIR (1964-1992)

Hafiz Akdemir had been working only briefly as a reporter with the Özgür Gündem newspaper when he was murdered with a shot from a pistol on the streets of Diyarbakir, the city where he was born, in the presence of his nephew. It was 8 June 1992. That same evening a deputy prime minister said on TV that the murder was the work of the PKK. Members of his family, friends and colleagues knew immediately that the state itself was behind the shooting. That was borne out officially years later when the culprits were arrested.

When he was murdered, Akdemir was 28 years old, although he had already spent eight years in prison at such a young age. In 1984, in the aftermath of the 1980 military coup, he was detained on suspicion of sympathising with the KÜK, a Kurdish nationalist organisation. He was found guilty and jailed until March 1991. He told his childhood friend and lawyer Sedat Cinar that he had begun working as a journalist after he was freed as 'training for getting accustomed to the new life'. Following his release in March he first had to spend three months recovering from a 52-day hunger strike while in prison.

In the approximately 20 days before the murder, there was a tension in the air that rose constantly, as the journalist Veysi Polat, Akdemir's nephew, recalls. One morning, as Veysi was walking to the newspaper offices with his uncle, as he frequently did, they found a letter on the door with the message: 'Your pen will break. It's your turn. Hizbullah-Kontra.' Hezbollah was a much feared death squad in the 1990s, linked to and probably even set up by the state. 'I think Hezbollah's eye had fallen on my uncle because he wrote about Hezbollah,' Polat told the Turkish news portal Bianet.org in 2011.

The shooting took place on a Monday morning as Hafiz and Veysi were on their way to the newspaper offices. Hafiz Akdemir was gunned down from behind. He was taken to Diyarbakir's university hospital, but succumbed to his injuries the same day. The state was able with ease to depict the murder as a settling of accounts among the Kurds. The deputy prime minister who spoke on TV that evening merely needed to repeat Akdemir's conviction for being a KÜK sympathiser to have the majority of Turks believing that the PKK had killed the journalist. It suited the image that many people had of the PKK at the time – and sometimes with justification – that the PKK dealt summarily with those allying themselves to other Kurdish organisations.

For eight years those responsible for the murder remained unidentified. But in 2000 the case finally came before the courts in a major case against a large gang of Hezbollah members. In the case, 31 Hezbollah members were on trial for a total of 188 murders, including that of Hafiz Akdemir. One of the accused, Fuat Balca, said that he had been a lookout at the murder of Akdemir, that a certain Mahmut Kaya had ordered the murder and provided the weapon, and that a man with the code name Hüseyin, real name Cihan Yildiz, had pulled the trigger.

In 2009, Balca received a life sentence along with 16 others. But because an appeal was launched, and suspects could not be held for longer than 10 years without being finally convicted, he was released in 2011. A little later the sentence was confirmed, and the court issued an arrest warrant for Balca, but by then he was nowhere to be found. Kaya was never brought to justice, as he was killed in a shootout with the police in Istanbul in 2000.

Cihan Yildiz was detained in Austria in 2007 and extradited to Turkey. During the trial he acknowledged being a past member of Hezbollah, but he denied being Akdemir's murderer.

METIN GÖKTEPE (1968-1996)

In the morning of the day of his death, 8 January 1996, photojournalist Metin Göktepe left for Istanbul's Alibeyköy Cemetery. Two men, Riza Boybas and Orhan Özen, who were being buried there, had been active in Turkey's leftist movement and had been beaten to death by the police during a prison riot. Göktepe was to have taken photographs. But the entire area around the cemetery had been cordoned off, and the police detained around a thousand mourners before they were able to reach the cemetery. Metin Göktepe was one of them. Those detained were taken to a sports hall, where they were maltreated. Precisely what happened to Göktepe during the course of the day has never been fully cleared up, but the same evening a phone call was made, by someone who has still not been identified, to Evrensel, the leftist newspaper set up in 1995 where he had been working for less than a year. This man reported that he had been detained with Göktepe that day and had been released, but that he knew that Göktepe had been so badly maltreated by the police that he had not survived.

The newspaper decided to publish the information. A statement from the state prosecutor followed to the effect that Göktepe had been released by the police and had been found hours later lying dead some 100 metres from the sports hall. It later emerged that the body had been found right next to the sports hall, and the autopsy showed that Göktepe had died as a result of internal bleeding, including a brain haemorrhage, caused by the repeated use of force. Three days later the Interior Minister at the time, Teoman Ünüsan, said on TV: 'I do not have all the information on this subject. However, according to my most recent information, Metin Göktepe died as a result of falling off a wall.'

The minister was forced to withdraw his statement under pressure from Göktepe's colleagues and the autopsy report. He offered an apology to Fadime Göktepe, Metin's mother, but she refused to accept it, and demanded that the guilty be punished. Fadime later said in an interview that she had never been able to read the newspaper that Metin, the seventh of her eight children, worked at. She said: 'My parents never allowed their children to go to school. Metin sent me on a course to learn to read. I went twice, and then I was able to write my name. That was enough, but he didn't agree of course. He laughed at me on one occasion when he said he would report me to the police if I didn't go to the course. I wish I had learned to read as a child.'

A legal case was made against 10 police officers alleged to have been involved in Göktepe's murder. Five of them were acquitted in 1999, while the others were sentenced to 18 years in prison. However, the sentence was reduced to seven years, on the grounds of good behaviour during the trial and because it was not clear in the judge's view precisely who had delivered the fatal blows. In 2000, the murderers were released under an amnesty, just one year and eight months after their conviction.

CHAPTER 3

INDEPENDENT MEDIA

Are there absolutely no media that have been able to evade this suffocating entanglement between media, commerce and politics that kills journalistic effort?

Yes there are, and they have been mentioned previously as havens for columnists fired by other media. Taraf (Side), Sözcü (Spokesperson) and Cumhuriyet (Republic) are the best known. Cumhuriyet is the oldest of the three, established in 1924, a year after the Turkish republic was founded. It has an illustrious history during which it has defended the secular foundations of the republic to the full. Taraf and Sözcü both saw the light of day in 2007. Taraf took on the task of harrying the army – and was an ally of the AKP government in its early years, when it wanted to curb the army's power. Sözcü has been staunchly opposed to the AKP since its first day on the newsstands.

Sözcü has now risen to become the third largest newspaper in Turkey after Hürriyet and Zaman, with a print run of around 340,000. By comparison: Taraf sells around 51,000 newspapers a day (and declining), Cumhuriyet around 53,000 (and growing).

The fact that these newspapers are not part of a major concern makes them independent, as they are not needed as part of a business strategy or to placate the government. Cumhuriyet will not miss out on a tender in the telecoms sector if it prints a scoop that Erdogan does not like. The editor of Sözcü can take on columnists who have been fired, as he does not have a cable or window frame division that would miss out on a contract to a TOKI complex being constructed.

The daily Zaman (Time) has a separate spot, along with the English edition – which has a separate news team and a more liberal approach than the Turkish Zaman – Today's Zaman. They too are not part of a large concern active in all sorts of other sectors. However, with respect to content and target group they cannot be compared with the popular new Sözcü and the old and journalistically established Cumhuriyet. Zaman is aimed at religious conservatives. 'That makes us a greater threat to the government than Sözcü or Cumhuriyet,' says Bülent Kenes, editor of Today's Zaman up until the end of 2015, speaking in a phone interview from the newspaper's offices in Istanbul in January 2016. 'Sözcü and Cumhuriyet readers are by definition far from the AKP, whereas our readers come from the same socio-economic group as AKP voters. The information that we provide our readers with and our op-eds could cause doubt among AKP voters, draw them away from the party. We are also big, in fact Turkey's second newspaper, after Hürriyet and ahead of Sözcü.'

On 4 March 2016, after a court order, trustees were appointed at Zaman and Today's Zaman, and many editors and columnists were fired, including Bülent Kenes. Zaman has now become a government mouthpiece.

The Zaman newspapers are part of the Hizmet (Service) movement, as they refer to themselves, or the movement of the Islamist cleric Fethullah Gülen, who lives in the United States. Fethullah Gülen and Tayyip Erdogan were close associates for years. Erdogan was a rising star in the Islamist party led by the father of Turkish political Islamism, the Welfare Party's Necmettin Erbakan, and a successful mayor of Istanbul between 1994 and 1998. During those years Gülen preached in the mosques of Turkey's major cities, garnering increasing support with his message on education, dialogue between religions and the responsibility of the Islamist community in rendering 'service' in the wider interest of society. The Hizmet movement is broad, for instance setting up banks and insurance companies during those years, as well as many schools and preparatory schools. . Photographs from the time show Gülen and Erdogan standing together like brothers, sometimes with political standard-bearers. Gülen and Erdogan were both controversial figures in those days. Gülen was being prosecuted because he was alleged to have wanted to undermine the secular state and left for the US in 1999, while Erdogan was imprisoned for four months that year for reciting an Islamist poem that the court saw as inciting hatred and violence.

The AKP, founded in 2001, won the 2002 elections easily and was able to form a government on its own. The fact that they have been able to remain in power for so long is, according to many people, thanks to collaboration with the Gülen movement. The suspicion was that the Gülencis, as Gülen's followers are often referred to, gained the opportunity via the AKP to occupy all sorts of positions in for example the judicial system and within the police. According to the movement's opponents, the ultimate goal of the Gülencis has always been to take over the state from within. And the fact is that an increasing number of religious people were appointed to positions in the state apparatus. But is that a problem? Should religious people have no right to a career as a civil servant? Was the aim really to turn Turkey into an Islamist state? No proof has ever been provided, but many people within and outside Turkey are fully convinced of this.

Whatever the case, feelings between Gülen and Erdogan cooled over the years, and on 17 December 2013 the final break came with a bang. On that day 52 people, including the director of a state bank (who had millions in cash kept in shoeboxes at home), an extremely wealthy Iranian businessman and various family members of ministers in Erdogan's cabinet, were arrested on charges of fraud, corruption, illegal gold transactions and money laundering. Further arrests were to follow later that month, and Erdogan's sons Bilal and Burak were named as suspects, but there was never a follow up to the investigation and no new arrests followed. Senior police officers, all quickly appointed after 17 December, were said to have refused to carry out orders issued by the public prosecutor. The prosecutor involved was replaced.

Erdogan was able to defuse the investigation quickly by transferring hundreds of police officers, including heads of department for financial and organised crime, and dismissing crucial prosecutors or reappointing them to positions from which they were unable to damage the government. He played down the investigation into embezzlement as a 'legal coup', carried out by Fethullah Gülen's followers, who were subsequently branded as 'terrorist'. A number of ministers named as being involved in corruption were replaced. And in effect that was the end of the matter. Many media previously in the Gülen camp quickly changed sides. They are still independent in the financial sense, but instead of being on the side of those in power, they were suddenly in direct opposition to those in power.

_ Opposition newspapers as sweetener

What Bülent Kenes says about the readers of Sözcü and Cumhuriyet is true: they are by definition hostile to the AKP, and in this sense they are relatively harmless to the electoral power of the AKP and Erdogan. However, what not everyone realises is how useful these newspapers are to the government. By not cutting them down to size, for example by imposing huge tax fines, or even banning publications, he can boost his democratic image to his backers and the outside world. Look at what Sözcü is printing! Look at how keen Cumhuriyet is on stories aimed at damaging us! Erdogan can point to these publications to demonstrate his so-called goodwill towards the press. Opposition newspapers as sweetener.

Especially with Sözcü, hatred of Erdogan leaps out of the page. They also receive all kinds of leaks about the AKP and organisations and companies linked to the AKP, scoring interesting scoops on this basis regularly – which remain unread by AKP supporters as they do not read this newspaper. Cumhuriyet also opposes the AKP government and Erdogan in particular, using less sensationalist language than Sözcü and fewer screaming headlines. In other words, Cumhuriyet derives from a tradition of journalism, whereas Sözcü is rather a campaign sheet.

Taraf had its years of glory when it resisted the might of the army, and its influence and reach have declined considerably since the army has largely, though not entirely, returned to its barracks, playing a less important role on the political stage than previously. Some see Taraf's journalistic credibility as damaged by the scoop on the Ergenekon coup plans and the evidence that fell into the hands of the newspaper, which later turned out to have been largely forged, and for which Taraf has never accepted journalistic responsibility.

In addition, there are a number of smaller independent newspapers, of which Evrensel (Universal) and BirGün (One Day) are the best known. Evrensel was established in 1995. It reports a great deal on the Kurdish issue and on the life of workers, on the environment and on culture. A year after it was founded, one of Evrensel's journalists, Metin Göktepe, was murdered by the police – see his bio on page 42. The newspaper's print run is rising, especially since the Gezi protests in 2013, and is now at around 11,000.

BirGün is a bit newer: the first issue was published in 2004. The newspaper is financially independent, but ideologically linked to a small leftist party, the ÖDP, Özgürlük ve Dayanısma Partisi, or the Freedom and Solidarity Party. Hrant Dink was one of the columnists at the newspaper until he was murdered in January 2007 – see his bio on page 24. BirGün's print run is also rising and is now at around 28,000. Both newspapers express themselves clearly when it comes to politics, like every Turkish newspaper, but both do so without sensationalism and inflammatory language.

The larger independent newspapers naturally play an important role in Turkey. Sözcü's star has soared since the Gezi protests because it was the only newspaper to unambiguously take the side of the demonstrators. It lifted its tirades against Erdogan to unprecedented heights. It was in fact basically the only news medium that the Gezi demonstrators felt was listening to them, where they thought that the facts of the demonstrations and the way in which they were suppressed by the authorities were being reported, and that the newspaper took account of their feelings and ideas. The demonstrators were desperate for this, as they found scarcely any or no honest reporting elsewhere. Hordes of Gezi demonstrators, who had proudly adopted the abusive term 'capulcu' – plunderers – given them by Erdogan in a speech, gathered in front of the offices of the major broadcasters CNNTürk and NTV to make their objections known while waving banknotes. The mailboxes of newspaper editors overflowed with emails containing complaints and curses.

Indicative of the poor or non-existant reporting on Gezi, a documentary on penguins was broadcast by CNNTürk on the evening that the protests got out of hand. The issue came up in the documentary 'Persona Non Grata' on press freedom in Turkey (on YouTube with English subtitles).

Aydin Dogan, the chief of Dogan Holding, the owner of CNNTürk, maintained in this documentary that the penguin documentary had been a 'professional error' and revealed what happened that evening, and how he discovered that a penguin revolt had broken out among the Gezi demonstrators. Aydin Dogan in 'Persona Non Grata': 'It was not done on purpose. You have to realise that from around midnight all the programmes are broadcast automatically. This was the case that evening: the broadcast programme had been drawn up and the staff had all gone home. The next morning my youngest daughter and chairman of the board of management stormed into my office and asked what we were doing. I didn't understand her. She told me that we had broadcast documentaries.' Dogan laughs out loud and then continues: 'It was still early in the morning, and that was the point at which we realised what had happened. But it was a purely professional mistake, and it was definitely not done on purpose. At the time they said it was the government's intention, but I don't agree. Simply a professional error.'

It may well be the case that the evening went that way. That there was no newsroom meeting at which a decision was taken to remain completely silent on the way the police were running out of control in dealing with the demonstrators, and instead to dump a penguin colony on the cable. The point is that the demonstrators believed none of it. CNNTürk redeemed itself to some extent with a four-hour live broadcast of the the way Taksim Square near Gezi Park was cleared violently, when the square was enveloped in a cloud of teargas and there was a constant stream from the water cannon, but relations between the demonstrators and the mass media were never restored.

The *capulcus* could not see their point of view reflected in the reporting in newspapers and on TV, where they received no or scarcely any opportunity to get their ideas across, where raw police violence received little attention and the government was not asked critical questions. For example, during the early days of Gezi much greater attention was paid to Prime Minister Erdogan's visit to Egypt, Tunisia and Libya, where the Arab Spring was in full swing and where Erdogan, as self-appointed example of a democratic Islamist leader, was welcomed by cheering crowds.
More significant was the fact that never before have so many journalists and columnists been fired by the major newspapers, including those owned by Dogan, as in the summer of 2013. According to the Turkish union of journalists, 59 journalists lost their jobs as a result of their reporting on the protests. Twenty two were shown the door, and 37 were forced to resign. The 'Gezi dismissals' carried on for a long time. In 2014 Ridvan Akar lost his job at CNNTürk, after it had broadcast a documentary by him on Gezi and its aftermath. There had apparently been a complaint from the powers that be.

For some of the *capulcus*, many of whom had never really been involved in politics until the mass protests, the way that the media behaved was a real eye-opener. They had never realised how mendacious the bulk of the Turkish news media were under the influence of their entanglement with commerce and politics. In their anger at the traditional news providers and their total rejection of the AKP and Erdogan, they ran to the kiosk every day to buy Sözcü to keep abreast of the news and to see their views reflected. They also launched their own 'TV channel', even though they broadcast only over the internet and the programmes were amateurish: Capul TV. Halk TV (People's TV), allied to the largest opposition party the CHP, referred to as the Sözcü of the TV broadcasters, also recorded high viewing figures at the time.

_ Closely meshed network of reporters

Kurdish media are also financially independent. The main ones are Özgür Gündem (Free Agenda) and the Kurdish language Azadiya Welat (Free Country) and the TV channels MedNûce and Stêrk. Their predecessor, MedTV, was based in London after being set up in 1995, transmitting by satellite to people's homes. MedNûce and Stêrk now broadcast from Denderleeuw near Brussels in Belgium. Between 2000 and 2005, two new Kurdish news agencies were added, Dicle (the local name for the River Tigris) and Firat (Euphrates).

These media have their roots in the 1990s, in the Kurdish political movement. These were the worst years of the war between the PKK and the Turkish army. Soldiers, PKK fighters and civilians died in large numbers, and hundreds of extrajudicial executions were carried out, mainly by the Jitem death squads of the Turkish army. Many people were detained by the police and disappeared without trace, and thousands of Kurds were displaced as two to three thousand villages were burned to the ground by the army. Kurds fled to the cities in the region, with many also travelling further to larger cities in the south and west of Turkey, such as Adana, Mersin, Izmir and Istanbul. But the news was not published in Turkish newspapers or broadcast by Turkish TV. Turks seeing the Kurdish population in their cities increasing did not know any better than to see them as economic migrants.

There was no way for Kurds really to keep abreast of the news that affected them. You knew that your own village had been burned to the ground by the army, but many people had no clear picture of the scale on which these practices were occurring. What did Kurdish politicians think about this, and how were the politicians treated in fact? There was only one thing for the Kurds to do: organise their own media.

The Turkish media at the time were unable to report on what was happening in the south-east of the country, because an emergency had been declared over a large part of Kurdish territory, placing insurmountable restrictions on the press. The press often simply could not get into the area.

But it may be asked whether the Turkish news media would have carried out their task if the restrictions had not been in place. The bulk of the Turkish media, irrespective of which party they were allied to, or which company they were part of, are after all part of the established powers that do not question the existing political system. Whether a Turkish media organisation is right or left wing, has a conservative religious character or is strongly secular, they firmly believe, with exceptions, in the basic principles of the Turkish state, the most important of which are nationalism and the indivisible unity of the state. To cast doubt on the state, or the then all-powerful Turkish army, which was deeply trusted by the majority of the population, was completely unacceptable in every way. This principle also applies to the newspaper which is currently seen as extremely critical and the most journalistic in Turkey, namely Cumhuriyet. It has always been a strictly secular daily, very much on the side of the army, and has only begun to change markedly over recent years.

And if the Turkish media had reported, how would they have done so? Probably the way they do now on the current human rights violations in the Kurdish region: not at all or incompletely, or mendaciously and manipulatively.

The Kurdish media were able to build up a closely meshed network of reporters in no time at all, right into every province and town, often with reporters even in the smaller villages. But that did not mean that the Kurdish media were able to go about their work freely. On the contrary. The Kurdish media derive from the Kurdish political movement and, because this has arisen from the same grassroots as the PKK, which was set up in 1978, they align themselves closely with the PKK. Firat in particular is seen as a PKK mouthpiece, something that is true to a certain extent. For example, they have a direct line to the PKK leadership in the mountains in northern Iraq and publish all the organisation's press statements. MedNûce is also in fact allied to the PKK. A picture of PKK leader Öcalan adorns the front page of Özgür Gündem every day, and the same is true of Azadiya Welat.

But we would not be doing justice to the Kurdish media if we were to see them purely as 'PKK media', for the simple reason that they have always been much more than that. As stated, they arose from the need to distribute the news about the region and the people, because no one else was doing it. And that is what they still do, in the same way that Turkish newspapers are there for the Turks, Dutch newspapers serve the Dutch people, Thai newspapers the Thai people.

They continue to report from the roots of Kurdish society on what happens in Kurdistan. Their opinion pages comment on the news from the perspective of the Kurdish movement, and the cultural pages and programmes deal with Kurdish literature, music and theatre. Staying informed about Kurdish news through the traditional media is impossible, just as for instance English people would be deprived of news, background and opinion important to them without their national media. There is TRT6, the state channel broadcasting in Kurdish, but this is under the control of the government. If you follow both TRT6 and the media reporting from the perspective of the Kurdish movement, you will at least gain a decent picture of the different views on the news of the day, and on what they consider to be the significant news of the region.

_ Deep animosity

How does the government deal with these media that it is unable to manipulate economically? Mainly though court cases, at which journalists are on occasion jailed. Cumhuriyet editor Can Dündar and his Ankara bureau chief, Erdem Gül, received a huge amount of international attention at the end of 2015, but a case about which less is heard is that of Mehmet Baransu, a well known and the most controversial investigative journalist in Turkey, who works for Taraf.

Baransu has been in jail since March 2015 on suspicion of 'acquiring secret documents', 'setting up a criminal organisation' and 'producing, publishing and destroying documents related to the interests of the state'. The allegation has a lot to do with a major – and ultimately unproved – planned coup that he revealed in Taraf in 2010. The revelation turned out exceptionally well for the Erdogan government: the army's political power had to be cut back and the coup plans could be utilised for that. However, these were also the years when Erdogan was a close friend of Fethullah Gülen, who had broad support in Turkey at the time. Gülen and Erdogan worked together, and an increasing number of Gülencis were given jobs in the police and justice system, including influential positions. However, that friendship cooled, turning into bitter enmity, when the AKP turned on the Gülencis, including Mehmet Baransu.

It is certainly a strange case – for one thing, since when are coup plans state secrets?– and press freedom activists and his fellow journalists believe that Baransu has been jailed for entirely different reasons. Journalist and columnist Abdullah Bozkurt of Zaman, a newspaper allied to the Gülen movement, wrote on 13 March 2015: 'The Islamist government, which benefited from Baransu's revelations regarding the conspiracy in 2010, now wants to keep this investigative journalist behind bars, simply because he is continuing to expose the government's dirty secrets, from the corruption dossiers to the unconstitutional working methods of the security service.'

There are innumerable court cases brought against journalists working at independent newspapers. The newspapers themselves have no idea how many court cases are pending and do not even take the trouble to keep an accurate count. A Taraf journalist once said that it would be more convenient to furnish a room at the newspaper's offices as an interrogation and court room, as this would make going to the courts for questioning and hearings less time-consuming.

The smaller the newspaper, the more difficult it is for it to defend itself against attempts at intimidation by the authorities. Evrensel and BirGün are sometimes compelled to ask their readers for additional contributions in order to pay for court cases or to ensure distribution. Evrensel was even shut down for a few days on a number of occasions in 1999 and 2000. The problems began when PKK leader Öcalan was held in Kenya in 1999 and taken to Turkey and appeared to narrowly avoid the death penalty. Referring to Öcalan's stated desire for peace with Turkey, Evrensel dared to print the headline: 'Death penalty for desire for peace'.

Today's Zaman also has a lot of court cases pending, and for Bülent Kenes that was the reason for resigning at the beginning of December 2015 from his position as editor, which he had held since the newspaper was founded in January 2007. Speaking in a phone interview in January 2016, he said: 'How can I carry out my job as editor if I have to go to court time and time again to defend the newspaper or to be questioned? The pressure is simply too great. I didn't want the responsibility any more. Now I write my column, and I read books a lot, and we will wait until this time is over.' Almost a year earlier, Ekrem Dumanli, the editor of Zaman (the Turkish language version) was detained in his newsroom with a number of cameras filming the event. Hidayet Karaca, director of the Samanyolu Media Group of the TV channel of the same name, was also detained. Dumanli stayed in jail for only a few days, but Karaca was still in jail at the time of writing in February 2016.

Today's Zaman is published by Feza Journalism, a company with no commercial interests in sectors other than journalism, and which is independent in that sense. But that does not mean that the authorities are unable to damage the newspaper economically. Bülent Kenes: 'Our advertisers were pressured not to advertise with us any longer. As a result, our advertising income fell by around 80 per cent. Our list of subscribers is also declining sharply. Until recently we were the Turkish newspaper with the most subscribers, but around 70 per cent have left us.'

Newsstand sales have also declined, according to Kenes, partly because it is dangerous to be seen carrying Zaman or Today's Zaman. He says: 'As a civil servant you can't turn up to work with Zaman, because you are then 'parallel' and could lose your job,' in reference to Erdogan's characterisation of the Gülen movement as attempting to establish a 'parallel state' alongside the official one. Erdogan uses and abuses the term to counter allegations against the government, implying that everything that goes wrong in Turkey or with the AKP government is because of the 'parallels'. Erdogan also attributes Cumhuriyet's scoop on the MIT weapon transports to the parallels, alleging that Cumhuriyet staff collaborated with the parallels within the legal system to acquire the incriminating images.

How long can Today's Zaman, along with other media within Feza Journalism, such as Cihan news agency and the Turkish Zaman, hold out against declining advertising income and subscribers? Kenes declined to answer directly, saying only that 'it's still working for the present'. The Gülen movement is not known to be short of money, so there are possibly funds available. Whether those funds are sufficient to guarantee the continuing existence of Today's Zaman for the present is unclear. Bülent Kenes: ‹News media allied to the government are already printing columns about placing our newspapers under trusteeship. It could happen at any moment.›

Zaman and Today's Zaman were eventually placed under trusteeship on 4 March 2016, a few weeks after this interview. Also the affiliated Cihan news agency is now run by a government appointed trustee. They became pro-government overnight.

This is not merely hypothetical. This happened in September 2015 to the Koza Ipek Group, along with the Bugün and Millet newspapers linked to the group, as well as to the TV channels Kanaltürk and Bugün TV. The Koza Ipek Group is active in other sectors (including insurance, health care, tourism, mining, nutrition and a university) and so not only in journalism, and they are part of Fethullah Gülen's Hizmet movement. The images showing the way in which the company and the media were taken over were shocking. Administrators appointed by the court and accompanied by the police entered Bugün TV, as editorial and other staff protesting outside were fired on with teargas and water cannon and a number of journalists were taken into custody. The editorial policy of all the media taken over was immediately changed. From one day to the next, Bugün, Millet, Kanaltürk and Bugün TV turned pro-government.

The authorities justified the takeover of the Koza Ipek Group using Act 6415, which deals with countering the financing of terrorism. Investigation was said to have shown that Ipek Koza had financial links with FETÖ, or the Fethullah Gülen Terrorist Organisation. That is as surrealist as it sounds. The Gülen movement, a religious and social organisation whose members have never been seen with weapons but rather with schoolbooks and the Koran, has been characterised by the Turkish authorities as 'terrorist'. This facilitates the use of all sorts of laws against the latest opponent of the AKP.

Koza Ipek's lawyers denied that there was anything wrong with the company's books, saying that the investigation by the tax inspection accountants and other authorities had found no irregularities at all in the two years before the appointment of trustees. Suddenly a lot that was not in order had been found in the most recent investigation by the Finance Ministry's financial crimes investigation council, they said. There is doubt about the independence of this report, just as there is about the judge who ordered the company to be placed under trusteeship. The AKP exercises power over the ministry, and the legal system has long ceased to be independent of the political rulers. Legal objection to the takeover was raised, but that was hopeless from the start.

_ Bomb attack

Suppression of the Kurdish media has been total from the time they were set up right up to today. All available means were used to silence Özgür Gündem and Azadiya Welat, and later the Dicle and Firat news agencies. The Turkish authorities also did all in their power to shut down Kurdish TV channels broadcasting from Europe, with RojTV being the most famous.

But they have never succeeded in silencing the Kurdish media. The Kurdish movement is too well organised, and too determined in its struggle for full political and cultural rights for the Kurds. Tussles with European authorities did not help in shutting down MedTV, RojTV or the other broadcasters from Europe that reach so many Kurds in Turkey and the surrounding countries.

Turkey continues to pressure European governments to deprive Kurdish channels of their broadcasting licences, frequently with success. For example, the UK's Independent Television Commission revoked the licence of the first Kurdish satellite broadcaster MedTV in April 1999, alleging that it was inciting crime and would lead to the disruption of public order. In 2004 a French judge withdrew the licence of the successor MedyaTV, citing 'links with the PKK'. Its successor, RojTV, has since broadcast with a Danish licence, leading to pressure for years from Turkey for Denmark to revoke the licence. Denmark has not gone that far, but it has, like other European authorities, imposed huge fines on the broadcaster. The last fine dates back to 2012, when a Danish court imposed a fine of as much as 5.2 million Danish krone (894,800 dollars) on RojTV for 'terrorist propaganda'. There are currently two Kurdish news broadcasters, Stêrk (Star) and Nûce (News), broadcasting with a Danish licence. The studios are in Denderleeuw near Brussels, where police have made several raids in the past.

How Kurdish newspapers fare is shown by the 14 names that Özgür Gündem has appeared under over the years, sometimes as daily and sometimes during times of financial need as weekly. Özgür Ülke, Yeni Ülke, Özgür Bakis and Ülkede Özgür Gündem are examples. The newspaper was first banned in 1994, two years after being founded. For a time in 1993 the newspaper did not appear for lack of money, and at the end of that year more than 100 reporters and other staff were arrested during raids on its offices in Istanbul, Diyarbakir, Izmir, Adana and other cities. The senior editors were given long prison sentences and left to go abroad. Of the 580 issues published up until closure in April 1994, 486 were confiscated.

On 3 December 1994 the offices of Özgür Ülke, Özgür Gündem's successor, were the targets of bomb attacks in Istanbul and Ankara. It was soon clear that the Turkish state was behind the attacks. At the end of November 1994, Prime Minister Tansu Ciller signed a document of the National Security Council (a consultation forum between the army and the government that still exists and which the army dominated in those years) calling for Özgür Ülke to be 'eliminated', in the words of the secret document that was ultimately made public. 'When I stood looking at the fire that was caused by the bomb, I thought that the newspaper was finished,' Özgür Gündem editor Hüseyin Aykol said in an interview in Ankara in 2012. But my colleagues phoned me to tell me where they were. Other independent newspapers made their facilities available to continue publishing the newspaper.' And so Özgür Ülke was on sale the day after the attack. It was a newspaper of just four pages with the front page headline: 'This fire will burn you too'.

One member of staff died in the blasts, and 23 were injured. During the history of the Kurdish media, more than 20 columnists, reporters and delivery staff have been murdered in total, and in most cases these murders remain unsolved. The most recent victim is a journalist from Azadiya Welat (Free Country), the sole Kurdish language newspaper in Turkey: Rohat Aktaş died in the basement of a building in Cizre on 24 February 2016, where he was reporting on fighting between the Turkish army and youth groups linked to the PKK. He was wounded and stayed behind with a group of people in a severely battered building that the emergency medical services were unable to reach as a result of constant firing.

There are innumerable court cases running against Özgür Gündem journalists, with lengthy sentences called for and handed down. The Committee to Protect Journalists (CPJ) stated in 1996 that Kurdish media were the victim of a 'coordinated campaign of arrests, bans and court cases'. Things have in fact changed since then. The newspaper is no longer banned at the drop of a hat – even if the most recent ban lasting a couple of days in 2013 is not that long ago – and the number of Kurdish journalists being murdered has declined since the 1990s. But the number of court cases is still considerable. Of the 32 journalists currently in Turkish prisons, the majority are Kurds, and the KCK case against 44 journalists for 'membership of a terrorist organisation', 'propaganda for a terrorist organisation' and even 'leading a terrorist organisation' is ongoing.

Özgür Gündem's editor in chief Hüseyin Aykol sees a direct line running from the bombings in 1994 to prosecution of Kurdish journalists today.

'Those people trying to muzzle these media are the same,' he says. At the end of November 1994 it was Prime Minister Tansu Ciller. In 2011, when the arrests in the KCK case started, it was Erdogan who openly acknowledged that he wanted to halt Kurdish politics, journalism and activism.' Erdogan was still prime minister at the time. Addressing the legal authorities – then widely assumed to be dominated by Gülen supporters – he said in public: 'Deal with them legally, and then we will take them on in parliament.'

UGUR MUMCU (1942-1993)

Ugur Mumcu worked as an investigative journalist at the daily Cumhuriyet. When he left his Ankara home on the morning of 24 January 1993 and started his car, a bomb exploded. He was killed instantly.

No one has ever been found guilty of his murder. There are numerous theories regarding where the perpetrators are to be found, all linked to the investigative projects that Mumcu worked on over the period leading up to his murder.

One of the issues he was investigating was links between Kurdish nationalists and the MIT Turkish intelligence services. A large quantity of weapons from the Turkish army were said to have fallen into the hands of Peshmerga fighters under Jalal Talabani, one of the Kurdish leaders in northern Iraq, which was at the time semi-autonomous from Iraq under Saddam Hussein. He was also said to be working on a story about MIT infiltrators in the armed Kurdish group, the PKK.
The state is believed to want to keep all this information secret and to have commissioned Jitem – a banned Turkish army death squad that carried out a string of murders during the 1990s, primarily in Turkey's largely Kurdish south-east – to kill Mumcu. Veli Küçük, a notorious Jitem boss, is said to have delegated the task to one of his associates, at least according to a well known Jitem member who later decided to talk.

Another theory turns on the involvement of the Israeli intelligence service, as the story about the Iraqi Kurdish leader Talabani that Mumcu was working on was linked to Israel: Israel supported Talabani in the 1990-1991 Gulf War. This is the theory of Ceyhan Mumcu, Ugur's brother, who has said that Ugur made contact with the Israeli authorities for his story.

Ugur Mumcu was born in Kirsehir in western Turkey and went on to study law in Ankara. While studying he began to write for leftwing media. From 1965 onwards he worked as a lawyer, and from 1969 he lectured for three years at the Legal Faculty where he had studied. Starting out with smaller leftist publications, he moved over the years to larger newspapers, such as Aksam, Cumhuriyet and Milliyet. At the start of the 1970s, before doing his compulsory military service, he was arrested on account of an article he had written that maligned the army, according to the authorities. He was sentenced to seven years in jail, spending almost a year in Ankara's notorious Mamak prison, where he was subjected to torture. A higher court threw the sentence out. After that he served his military time, after which he started working in 1974 as a columnist for the magazine Yeni Ortan. From 1995 he began working for Cumhuriyet. Mumcu became one of Turkey's most important investigative journalists, taking on sensitive dossiers. He won various journalistic prizes.

Ugur Mumcu was married to Güldal Mumcu, who was elected to parliament for the largest opposition party, the CHP, in the 2007 and 2011 elections. Ugur and Güldal Mumcu had two children: Özgür, a son and Özge, a daughter.

CHAPTER 4

THE LAW

As a rule TEM, the counter-terrorism unit of the Turkish police, bashes down the door at five in the morning to conduct a house search and to take someone into custody. For the author they chose a more amenable time. It was around half past 12 in the afternoon when there came a hammering at the door, which was opened by a somewhat irked journalist. Why hammer rather than ring the bell? A TEM team eight or nine strong stood there with weapons at the ready in the stairwell hall. There should be a film of the proceedings, because one of the officers recorded everything with a small camera, as is usually the case. On the film a journalist who is unable to utter a word for the first few minutes and observes the stairwell tableau with her mouth open in amazement. The TEM? Here? For me?

Propaganda for a terrorist organisation. That was what I stood accused of, the leader of the TEM team told me. And that was the reason for the house search that immediately got underway. I reacted with astonishment and anger. 'Terrorism? All I do is hold a pen! I have nothing to do with violence!' 'Calm down ma'am,' the TEM officer said. 'Calm down? Eight of you come into my home, you accuse me of terrorist propaganda and I have to act calm?'

At the same time I realised that it was actually good advice to behave calmly. After all, when have I ever had the opportunity as a journalist to experience a TEM house search live? I calmed down, saw that a couple of men were searching my workroom and took up a strategic position at the door post to take it all in properly.

A low, long cabinet stood in my workroom with books, bags and equipment, and a disorganised archive of a whole lot of paper: folders, stacks of notes leaning haphazardly, a disorganised mound of business cards, notebooks of all shapes and sizes scribbled full, you name it. I had to chuckle internally: what would they be able to do with all that? There was also a book, 'Kurdistan in the Shadow of History' by Susan Meiselas, the most beautiful book about Kurdistan ever published. A police officer paged through it and signalled to his colleague with the camera. I walked over calmly, curious about what their eye had fallen on. A photograph of PKK leader Öcalan. The camera zoomed in. Proof!

Not long afterwards the house search was called off. Don't ask me why. I haven't been able to find out. Perhaps it dawned on those who had ordered the operation that Dutch Foreign Affairs Minister Koenders was in the capital Ankara that day for an official visit. In any event, the TEM team leader received a phone call, after which the house search was halted. I quickly sent out a tweet and I was also able to inform the Dutch Consul General in Istanbul of my detention, after which the TEM took me to the van for detainees.

 The questioning at the police station was quite easy. Had I ever crossed a Turkish border illegally? No. Was it true that I had interviewed PKK leader Cemil Bayik in the Qandil Mountains in northern Iraq? Yes. Was I a member of any organisation? No. What did I share on Twitter with my followers? The news and my views on the news, links to my most recent articles and columns, and scenes and experiences from daily life – and that is for everyone to see, officer, for you too. I was taken to the state hospital before and after the visit to the police station. That is mandatory, and a measure to prevent the use of torture by the police. A doctor or paramedic checks your limbs, back and abdomen for injuries and bruises, and then checks after the interrogation at the station whether there are any new injuries or bruises.

Four or five hours after I had informed the consulate of my situation, I was home again, completely astonished at what had happened to me. I knew of course that the products of my pen were acerbic on occasion and criticism of the government harsh. I knew of course that the topic that I specialised in, the Kurdish question, was still extremely sensitive in Turkey. I knew of course that I had attracted added attention by being the only foreign correspondent based in Diyarbakir, the largest city in the Kurdish south-east. But I did not expect for a second that the authorities would send the police down on me. The last time that a foreign journalist was harassed in this way by the government was in the 1990s, when Aliza Marcus from the US and Andrew Finkel from the UK had to appear in court.

On the day of the house search and questioning, 6 January 2015, I did not yet know whether I would in fact end up in the dock, but in February I received a letter: I had to report to court on 8 April 2015.

So there I sat. Jeans, high heels, new black suede jacket, black scarf with glitter, fresh haircut. As sure of my case as I could be. My lawyer Ramazan Demir sat next to me bursting with just as much confidence. Behind me, at a considerable distance, as the court is of insane dimensions, were family, friends and colleagues. Three judges opposite me – this was the court for serious crime, so having just one judge was out of the question – the prosecutor next to the judges. The evidence was read out. The prosecutor had his say. Then it was up to me to present my defence. I did so in Turkish.

I based my case on my identity. That the prosecutor had cut paragraphs and sentences from my columns and articles and had in so doing presented them, torn completely out of their context, as propaganda for a terrorist organisation. That the learned prosecutor had thereby attempted to depict me as a propagandist, but that he had not succeeded in his intention, as this was an insult to my true identity as a journalist. A journalist who certainly presents her opinions in plain terms in her columns, but never simply voices something without backing it up with argument, as is proper for a professional journalist.

Every now and then I looked up from my documents at my judges. One of them watched leaning forward in attention with her mouth open. What did that mean? I admit that I hoped for a little admiration for my Turkish and the content of my defence, but it could also well have been complete amazement at and rejection of my plea. I guess it was the first: after a few days of considering the evidence, the judges came to the conclusion that what I had written fell under freedom of expression. Acquittal. Everything pointed that way during the session. Even the prosecutor – a different prosecutor than the one who had taken the decision to prosecute and who had prepared the charge – called for acquittal that day in April.

The case is still ongoing by the way. Not long after the verdict my lawyer Ramazan phoned me to say that the prosecutor had lodged an appeal against the acquittal. It could take some time before a verdict was handed down, at least until the spring of 2016, he said. Bright spot: an appeal like this was largely routine and said nothing about the legal soundness of the verdict. This also emerged from the opinion of one of the three judges, who dissented from the acquittal and in his supporting argument did not get beyond stating that he did not agree. Appeals in Turkey are dealt with at an administrative level, so I do not have to appear in person again before a court.

The case naturally kept me busy, especially in the sense that it took up a great deal of time and brainpower. The innumerable interviews about it that I have given. The defence that I had to write and that had to be as solid as a rock. Consultation with legal advisers from the Dutch journalists' trade union (NVJ) and going over the case with my lawyer. The afternoon at the police station, the morning in the court in Diyarbakir.

But I did not sleep badly for even one night, if I recall well. I was scarcely worried at all about the outcome of the case, simply because I knew that I was doing my work in good conscience. Of course there are a lot of journalists in Turkey in jail who also did their work in good conscience, but for me what counts most is my own professional integrity. A conviction would not mean that I had suddenly become a propagandist. A conviction would, to stick to the idea behind my defence, not undermine my identity as a journalist, even if they had thrown me into jail. Turkey does not have that kind of power over me.

_ Bicycle loaded with newspapers

What I gladly made use of in each interview about my case was the opportunity to draw attention to the fate of many of my Turkish, and more especially Kurdish, colleagues.

And that fate is a hard one. There were around 32 journalists in prison in Turkey while I was writing this book. The 'around' is a bit strange, because you would think you could just count them, but it is unfortunately not that easy. The Committee to Protect Journalists (CPJ) for instance, says that on 1 December 2015 there were just 14 journalists in jail, while the International Federation of Journalists (IFJ) counted 30. Certain organisations for instance include publishers and managers of media companies in their count, while others do not, and whether the journalistic work of the journalist is used against them is sometimes also taken into consideration. Some of those keeping count in Turkey itself arrive at a figure higher than 32, because for example they count people detained for distributing newspapers as well, whereas these people are not counted by others as they do not work as journalists. Including those delivering newspapers should however not be seen as an attempt to boost the number of journalists in prison for propaganda reasons. It always concerns those delivering Kurdish newspapers such as Özgür Gündem and Azadiya Welat, for they are seen as full-fledged media workers. This is rooted in history. During the 1990s, when these newspapers were banned, those distributing them risked their lives. They were detained, tortured and even murdered for the work that they did out of conviction. The most recent murder of a newspaper distributor was not that long ago. On 14 October 2014, Kadri Bağdu, who was delivering the Kurdish language Azadiya Welat, was shot dead on the street in Ceyhan in southern Turkey while on his bicycle loaded with newspapers. His murder has so far not been solved.

The number of journalists in prison is always a snapshot – the figures could be different by the time this book goes to press. Online lists kept by international journalist organisations are often out of date and are not always updated with each release or arrest. This has partly to do with long detention on remand in Turkey that can run to five years. In principle you could be released from custody on remand, and lawyers are also constantly serving applications for their clients' release. The days when the courts are in session, which could be months apart under the Turkish justice system, are often the most significant times. For example, in March 2014 the number of journalists in prison fell suddenly when eight suspects were released in a major case against dozens of journalists. In May the same year, another seven journalists were released from prison in the same case. Meanwhile, the trials of these mainly print journalists continue.

The number of convicted journalists is equally difficult to ascertain. Who counts as a journalist, and who does not? The fact is that a number of journalists are serving life sentences. For example Hatice Duman, owner and editor of the socialist magazine Atilim (Leap), who was detained in 2003. She was ultimately convicted in 2011 and sentenced to life for membership of the banned Marxist-Leninist party MLKP, producing propaganda and attempting to overthrow the constitutional order. According to the CPJ, the allegations are unfounded. She could be held on remand for so long because the maximum number of years for being held without conviction was reduced from ten to five years only in 2014.

Mustafa Gök, Ankara correspondent for the leftist magazine Ekmek ve Adalet (Bread and Justice), is also serving a life sentence. He was detained in 2004 and convicted twice over. He received six years for membership of the banned Revolutionary People's Liberation Party-Front (DHKP/C) and life for membership of a terrorist organisation, a bomb attack, murder and fraud. The CPJ writes that according to Gök's lawyer, the evidence consists of stories that he wrote as a journalist and his presence at demonstrations. Gök has a brain disease that is deteriorating by the day, but the authorities don't consider his disease to be good enough reason for his release.

Erdal Süsem, who set up and edited the leftist cultural magazine Eylül Sanat Edebiyat Dergisi (September Art Literature Magazine), was detained in 2010 for propaganda for the banned Maoist Communist

Party. The case is still ongoing, and he could get 15 years. He was jailed previously on a charge of stealing a weapon from a police officer that was subsequently used to commit murder. Süsem denied the allegations, and the Constitutional Court ruled that there was insufficient evidence. However, when he was detained in 2010, the old allegations were raised again and a life sentence was the result. The case is currently before the European Court of Human Rights (ECHR).

Seyithan Akyüz, a reporter for Azadiya Welat detained in 2009, was sentenced to 12 years for membership of a terrorist organisation (i.e.: the PKK). The evidence was possession of banned newspapers and attending a demonstration in the western city of Izmir. Kenan Karavil, editor of Radyo Dünya (Radio World), was accused of being a member of terrorist organisations, namely the PKK and the KCK (a Kurdish umbrella organisation). He was detained in 2009 and sentenced to 25 years. The evidence, according to the authorities, who shared the information with the CPJ, consisted of news programmes that Karavil had made, meetings with members of the Kurdish DTP party – which no longer exists following a 2011 ban – and taped conversations with colleagues, listeners, sources and his lawyer.

Then there is Mehmet Baransu, one of Turkey's most famous investigative journalists, who was detained in 2015. The same year he received a 10month jail sentence for defaming President Erdogan in a series of tweets sent in 2013, some of which were sent from a Twitter account that was not even his, according to his lawyer. Short sentences like this are normally automatically suspended in Turkey, and Baransu should thus be free. But he is still being held on remand for much more significant allegations: being in possession of secret documents and membership of a terrorist organisation. He could still be handed a prison sentence of at most eight years for this.

Anyone closely following the news on journalism in Turkey will disturbingly often come upon reports that a journalist has been taken into custody yet again. But these men and women, mostly Kurds working for Kurdish media, are often released the same day or after at most four days.

In Turkey detained persons have to appear before the public prosecutor at the latest on the fourth day after being held. The prosecutor then decides whether the detainee will be formally arrested. Only if that happens do you count as a journalist in jail.

_ In line with European standards

By far the law most frequently used against journalists is Act 3713, the counter-terrorism legislation. Both the European Union and human rights organisations like Amnesty International and Human Rights Watch have criticised this law for years, saying that it is too broad in scope and criminalises not only peaceful activism but even the normal exercise of their profession by journalists, lawyers, politicians and others. Article 1 defines terrorism in this way: 'Terrorism is any kind of act done by one or more persons belonging to an organization with the aim of changing the characteristics of the Republic as specified in the Constitution, its political, legal, social, secular and economic system, damaging the indivisible unity of the State with its territory and nation, endangering the existence of the Turkish State and Republic, weakening or destroying or seizing the authority of the State, eliminating fundamental rights and freedoms, or damaging the internal and external security of the State, public order or general health by means of pressure, force and violence, terror, intimidation, oppression or threat.'

There follows a whole series of activities that may be deemed terrorism and that are also vaguely defined. For example Article 7 of Act 3713: 'Anyone engaging in propaganda for a terrorist organisation will be sentenced to prison for between one and five years.' This is the law that was used against me and for which they arbitrarily shopped around in columns that I wrote for the independent Turkish news portal Diken (Thorn). I think that I drew the attention of the authorities also as a result of these almost weekly publications in Turkish. Even a column in which I suggested Kurdish identity was evolving through the Kurdish struggle for more rights, for example by making Kurdish identity largely political and as a result fairly one-sided; this article was inflated into so-called propaganda What is meant precisely by 'propaganda' is not set out in the act and so it could be anything: my columns, or for example reporting on a demonstration where PKK slogans are shouted, or attending a political meeting of a Kurdish party. Many journalists who have been prosecuted for engaging in propaganda for a terrorist organisation were not convicted because the European Court for Human Rights has handed down clear rulings on freedom of expression and Turkey has to adhere to these rulings, but this does not stop Turkish prosecutors from mounting cases of this kind. After all, in this way journalists can still be intimidated and kept from doing their work.

A few years ago the law was amended, bringing the act further into line with European standards, according to the government. For instance, the previous provision that anyone engaging in propaganda for a terrorist organisation was automatically a member of the organisation and had to be prosecuted for this as well, was deleted. It is a pity though that in practice it did not make a great deal of difference. The term 'membership' is also not specified in the counter-terrorism law, which means that if you want to secure a conviction, you can lay a charge of membership of a terrorist organisation on the basis of articles written. Or of committing a crime in the name of an organisation without being a member of that organisation, and those convicted of crimes of this kind are then punished as members of that organisation under Article 2 of Act 3713.

The problem is not just the act itself, but also the fact it is being used increasingly often against people who have not used any violence at all. Emma Sinclair-Web, Turkey specialist at Human Rights Watch, cited the official figures when she told Voice of America at the end of 2013: 'According to official figures of the Justice Ministry, in the last four years an enormous number of people – somewhere around 40,000 – have been prosecuted for membership of armed organizations, and half of them have received convictions under that law. Now it applies disproportionately to Kurds in Turkey, but it also applies to other groups: it has been used against leftists, it has been used against journalists, students, for activities which could not in any way be counted as terrorism.'[3]

_ A joint project

How this works in practice is shown by a huge case brought against more than 40 journalists, the so-called KCK press case. Most of the accused in the case were detained at the end of 2011 and beginning of 2012, with the last being released in May 2014, although the case continues. As all the accused have been released pending a verdict, there is currently no longer much interest in the case, but that does not diminish the absurdity of it. The KCK is a Kurdish umbrella organisation, with the PKK as part of it and with the imprisoned PKK leader Öcalan as its president.

Most of the court sessions are being held in Istanbul, initially in a fairly small courtroom, but on the last few occasions in a huge space that has been specially built for mass trials with many suspects. Reading out the evidence was a never-ending exercise, which on occasion led to a chuckle from the accused and from the public gallery because of its craziness. The prosecutor attempted to show that the accused gathered in the court were members of a terrorist organisation and that some of them even provided leadership, using tapped phone calls that contained nothing in reality to indicate terrorist activity. For example they concerned attendance at a meeting ('Who's coming? Is someone taking something to eat?') or sharing and delegating editorial duties ('Who is going to the demonstration, who is going to the court?') and even about grocery shopping, of which the prosecutor suggested, without providing a shred of evidence, that the tomatoes asked for were a code word for explosives. The court sits in the KCK press case once every few months, and there is still a chance that some of the accused could be convicted. Moreover the case, which is part of the much larger KCK case, where Kurdish politicians, mayors, activists and even lawyers are in the dock, is seen as a joint project

3 http://www.voanews.com/content/turkey-anti-terror-law-casts-increasingly-wide-net/1772399.html

of the governing AKP party and Fethullah Gülen's religious movement, which were still close allies in 2011 and 2012. The Gülen supporters, so-called Gülencis, at the time allegedly occupied senior positions in the justice system and had the power to tackle the Kurdish political movement through the justice system, and were given the opportunity to do so by the AKP government. Gülen newspapers persisted in their support for the KCK cases in those years, even those against their fellow journalists.

But what in fact is a 'terrorist organisation'? There has been an international discussion for decades about the definition, but what many definitions have in common is that terrorists make use of violence and use weapons to do this. This is not the case in Turkey. There everyone runs the risk of being declared a terrorist, even if they belong to an organisation or show sympathy for an organisation not engaged in armed struggle. Turkey has seen the advent of yet another terrorist organisation since conflict broke out at the end of 2013 between the AKP ruling party and Fethullah Gülen's movement. This is FETÖ, the Fethullah Terör Örgütü, the Fethullah Terror Organisation. Now, one can say anything about the Gülencis, but not that they have ever taken up arms, nor that their leader has ever made use of anything to disseminate his teachings other than the Koran and a pen. The government's reasoning is that the Gülencis tried to topple the government through a 'judicial coup', and mounting or trying to mount a coup is equivalent to terrorism in the eyes of the government. And so FETÖ was suddenly a reality in 2014.

Counter-terrorism legislation has since been used against journalists linked to the Gülen newspapers, and against everyone suspected of being in league with them, for example Cumhuriyet editor Can Dündar and the newspaper's Ankara correspondent Erdem Gül. After all, the MIT arms transports to Syria were intercepted on the orders of prosecutors accused by the government of being Gülen supporters – appointed to their positions when the AKP and the Gülencis were still allies – and subsequently the incriminating evidence found in the trucks fell into the hands of Cumhuriyet. The fact that Cumhuriyet has long been a strictly secular newspaper with editors and columnists who would have nothing to do with the Gülen movement, and even warned of its dangers, makes the entire issue even sillier.

Legally it cannot be proved, but it is important that Cumhuriyet's story about the MIT trucks needs to be judged on its journalistic merits, not through prosecution in the courts. Have they evaluated and checked the film footage on a journalistic basis? Do they know precisely who their sources (whose identity they cannot reveal in accordance with journalistic ethics) are and whether they are reliable? Are other sources able to confirm the story? In a healthy journalistic climate, the media would try to answer these questions and dive deeper into the MIT trucks case, and if there were a way to view government documents, they would use this procedure to bring more information to light.

Nothing of the kind happens in Turkey. Cumhuriyet is dismissed as a treasonous newspaper and the two imprisoned staff members as spies and allies of terrorists. In any case, Can Dündar knew how to handle the allegation after he was detained and spoke briefly to HalkTV, a station linked to the CHP opposition party: 'For us this matter is a badge of honour.'

Can Dündar and Erdem Gül were released in the very early hours of Friday 26 February 2016. Turkey's Constitutional Court had ruled that their detention was violating their rights. The court case against them continues. President Erdogan has stated that he does not accept nor respect the Court's ruling.

The counter-terrorism legislation must be abolished or at least thoroughly revised in order to give press freedom a chance in Turkey. But that certainly wouldn't solve the problem. Another major obstacle is Clause 28 in the constitution. It starts full of hope with: 'The press is free and shall not be censored.' But then it goes off the rails with almost 400 words of restrictions. Here too, protecting the state is the priority, with repeated phrases such as 'internal and external security of the state', 'indivisible integrity of the state', 'state secrets'. It also refers to judicial orders when confiscating newspapers and magazines for instance, but because the judicial system is almost totally under the government's control, that can scarcely be seen as a democratic check.

Press freedom is restricted by Article 3 of the Press Act 5187, which starts just as full of hope with the statement that the press is free. It continues: 'This freedom includes the right to gather and disseminate information, and the criticism, interpretation and creation of work.' But it adds: 'The exercise of this freedom can be restricted in accordance with the requirements of a democratic society in order to protect the reputation and rights of others, and public health and morals, national safety and public order and safety; to safeguard the indivisible integrity of its territory; to prevent crime; to withhold information characterised as a state secret; and to guarantee the authority and impartial functioning of the legal system.'

What if the government wants to prevent certain news stories from coming out and being circulated? Then they make a judge or RTÜK (see further down for more info) issue a media ban on the specific story. This tool is used a lot, and again, the MIT transport that Cumhuriyet reported on is an example. The stories of the MIT trucks started to circulate in early 2014, as the trucks were raided on the orders of a prosecutor. Soon a judge banned the story from being reported, and the news faded away.

There are countless examples of this. The Roboski massacre (see Chapter 2) is an example in the first hours after it happened. And reporting the aftermath of a bombing in May 2013 in Reyhanli, a town on the Syrian border, in which 51 people were killed, was forbidden after a court order. This court order was cancelled a few days later by a higher court, but the media had been silenced on the important news for days, and were clearly notified of what they should and should not broadcast. When officials visited wounded victims in hospital, the government decided which journalists were allowed to cover it.

Another famous example is the taking hostage of a prosecutor in a big court house in Istanbul, in March 2015. The leftist-Marxist DHKP-C captured the prosecutor and pointed a gun at his head, claiming he was responsible for not carrying out a proper investigation into the death of Berkin Elvan.

Berkin was a 15-year old boy who died after he was wounded by a teargas canister shot by police during the Gezi-protests in 2013, while he was out on the street to buy bread. The picture of the prosecutor with the gun against his head was designated 'terrorist propaganda', and thus banned. When the photo kept surfacing on social media, the government decided to close Twitter altogether.

And then the bombing in Ankara by the Kurdish splinter group TAK in February 2016; a news ban was imposed within fifteen minutes after it happened. On Twitter somebody said: 'They ban Twitter even before putting out the fire caused by the bomb'.

Other examples: in March 2014 the court ruled it was forbidden to share recordings of a secret National Security Council meeting. Two months later, in May, a tragedy unfolded in the West-Turkish town of Soma: a coal mine collapsed and 301 mine workers died. A court issued a ban on publications that could be 'disrespectful to feelings of the families of victims'. Many channels and papers didn't report much at all about this biggest mine incident in Turkey's history, since many people who knew the situation at the mine blamed the government for the tragedy: the mine owner was a friend of the AKP government who reportedly didn't care about miners' lives but only about profits, and was, those involved claimed, aided by the government which didn't have a proper work safety policy.

In June 2014, 49 employees of the Turkish consulate in Mosul in Iraq were kidnapped by Islamic State, and the media were banned from reporting it. When the employees were released in September 2014, the media could only report their release and were not supposed to ask why the consulate hadn't been secure enough or what the Turkish authorities exactly did to secure their release.

_ Military heritage

Many of these restrictions were included in the constitution and the legal code following the 1980 military coup. The military wrote the 1982 constitution, and that constitution remains in effect. It has been amended several times, most recently in 2010, when the constitutional amendments were approved by the electorate in a referendum. The date of the referendum was chosen symbolically: 12 September 2010, exactly 30 years after the military coup of 1980. The message was that the constitutional amendments effectively drew a line under the country's military heritage. But that was not the case.

The constitution's central idea has remained in place, and this turns on the notion that the state protects itself against its citizens, instead of the citizens against the state. Everyone in Turkey agrees that the constitution urgently needs revision, and all the parties in parliament gladly join commissions supposed to prepare a revision and carry it out, but the commissions never last long. The last collapsed in February 2016, when the largest opposition party, the CHP, left the constitutional negotiating table because, in its view, the AKP insisted on replacing the parliamentary system by a presidential system – something that the CHP, just as the other two opposition parties, the HDP and MHP, vehemently opposes.

RTÜK, the Radio and Television Supreme Council, was established in the 1990s and its operations regulated under the constitution and in other laws. In 1994 to be precise, the year that organisations other than the state for the first time gained the right to make TV and radio broadcasts. RTÜK monitors all broadcasts and imposes fines for the infringement of all kinds of standards. This concerns soap series and films (the channel that broadcast the film Sex and the City 2 was fined because it showed a gay wedding, something that was 'immoral' according to RTÜK) and also often journalistic programmes like talk shows on current affairs.

For example, CNNTürk was fined as much as € 225,000. in November 2015 because a guest in Ahmet Hakan's popular talk show, Tarafsız Bölge (Neutral Zone), said during a broadcast in October that he did not consider the PKK a terrorist organisation. RTÜK ruled that this was 'propaganda for a terrorist organisation'. The guest, the prominent

Kurdish lawyer and human rights activist Tahir Elci, was shot dead on the street late November, after his comments had unleashed a storm of criticism from AKP politicians among others.

According to the constitution, RTÜK is an independent, autonomous council, but in practice it is not: the nine members are chosen by parliament, with the number of delegates per party depending on the number of seats the party holds. The current chairman, Ilhan Yerlikaya, sat on the council from 2005, stood down between 2011 and 2015 to be a member of parliament for the AKP, and then returned to become chairman. Four RTÜK seats are held by the AKP, two each by the MHP and CHP, and one by the HDP. While the AKP does not have a majority, there is a majority for conservative-Islamist social values (represented primarily by the AKP and MHP) and for Turkish nationalism (represented by all parties other than the HDP).

And the same applies to newspapers which know very well where the borders are drawn: RTÜK does not have to impose a lot of fines to big stations, because radio and TV broadcasters know the boundaries and stay well within them. There is no question of free journalistic debate on TV any more, and fewer broadcasters now dare to invite guests who might say something controversial during prime time or live broadcasts.

_ Intimidating situation
On Saturday 5 September 2015 I was detained for the second time by the TEM, the counter-terrorism police. It happened near the town of Yüksekova in the far south-east of Turkey close to both the Iranian and the Iraqi borders. I had been to a valley in the area with a so-called 'living shield group', where the group wanted to prevent fighting between the army and the PKK. I was supposed to stay only for the afternoon, but I was offered a place in the women's tent, and staying for the night seemed a good idea for the report that I was planning.

One of the police officers shone his torch right in my face when looking through the minibus that I was sitting in with the group. 'Who are you?' 'Geerdink, foreign journalist,' I answered. It was a really intimidating situation with large automatic weapons in a minibus, and it went through my head that the presence of a foreign journalist could possibly be to the advantage of the group as a whole, and that they would treat us better than if no foreign eyes were on the situation. The officer, however, barked at me: 'What are you doing here interfering in our affairs? Isn't there enough news in your own country?'

After three nights in a cell, the entire group of more than 30 was taken to the palace of justice to make statements to the public prosecutor. A decision would then be taken as to whether we would be officially arrested or not, and as a result would have to remain in custody or not. The two lawyers representing the group believed that if I as a foreigner made my statement in Turkish, it would dispose the prosecutor more favourably, and so I did that. I thought that it might have helped a bit, because at the end of the afternoon I heard the news that I was to be released along with the five other women in the group. A little later the lawyer looked penetratingly at me. He said: 'It may well be that they will now deport you.' 'What? Now? Immediately?' I responded, and in a reflex I threw my arms around the column I was standing next to and locked my hands. It would take a strong police officer to get me away from there! I soon let go of the column of course. I was powerless and unable to have any further influence on what might follow. None of the lawyers could stay with me, because they had to go with the men, who were to be taken to prison, and with the women in order to deal with the formalities. They insisted that I should phone them if I needed them. I did in fact need them, but contrary to the rules I did not get permission to make a phone call. And so I went, first to Van airport to fly to Istanbul, and then, after a string of formalities and long delays, on a flight to Amsterdam. Two police officers, a man and a woman, accompanied me right up to the gate. They had me sign forms stating why I as a foreigner could no longer remain in Turkey. I was a danger to public health, public order and public safety.

While I await the outcome of the appeal in my first case, another case may be added. The public prosecutor in Yüksekova is considering the question whether the entire group that I was part of should be charged with 'assisting a terrorist organisation'.

At the end of January 2016 the charges against Can Dündar and Erdem Gül were published. The public prosecutor in Istanbul is calling for a life sentence, an aggravated life sentence and 30 years in jail on charges of acquiring and revealing state secrets for the purpose of espionage, attempting to overthrow the government and assisting an armed terrorist organisation.

NAJI JERF (1978-2015)

This is the only journalist in this biographical series who is not a Turkish citizen. He has a place here, because the number of murders of journalists in Turkey has increased again since the rise of ISIS in Iraq and especially in Syria. Turkey is becoming an increasingly dangerous country for journalists at this level as well.

At the end of October 2015, Ibrahim Abdulkader and Firas Hammadi were murdered in Sanliurfa, near the border with Syria. The Syrians both worked for the weekly Ayn Watan (Eye of the Nation), a publication linked to a group of journalists known as "Raqqa is Being Slaughtered Silently". Hammadi was in charge of the day-to-day management, and Abdulkader was a reporter. The weekly backed the Free Syrian Army (FSA), and according to members of their families the men came under threat on account of articles they had published attacking ISIS. The two were found with their throats cut in the apartment they were sharing. The police detained seven suspects.

Naji Jerf was the editor of the independent weekly Hentah and a documentary filmmaker. He had just finished a documentary on Raqqa is Being Slaughtered Silently. Before that he had made a film about Syrian activists murdered by ISIS in Aleppo. The film, entitled 'ISIL in Aleppo', may be seen on YouTube. On 27 December 2015 he was shot in the head and chest in front of a building housing Syrian opposition media in the centre of the southern Turkish city of Gaziantep. He died later in hospital. According to TV broadcaster Al-Arabiya, ISIS claimed responsibility for the murder in a statement. Turkish police are investigating the case.

The Committee for the Protection of Journalists (CPJ) said in reaction to Jerf's murder: 'Syrian journalists who have fled to Turkey for their safety are not safe at all.'

Naji Jerf was 37 years old and married with two children. It was to have been his last week in Turkey, as he had been granted asylum in France and was due to fly to Paris with his family a week later.

MUSA ANTER (1920-1992)

If there is anyone of significance for Kurdish journalism and literature, it is certainly Musa Anter, affectionately known to the Kurds as Apê Musa (Uncle Musa). His violent death in Diyarbakir on 20 September 1992 came as a shock to the Kurdish community in Turkey. His portrait – a calm elderly man with white hair – can be seen all over Turkey's Kurdish regions.

Musa Anter was born in a little village in Mardin Province in the south-east of Turkey. He studied law for a couple of years in Istanbul, but left university to write and to engage in politics. He was detained in 1959 because he had written a Kurdish poem, Qimil, for the newspaper Ileri Yurt. Publishing a poem in Kurdish was inconceivable at the time, but a movement was initiated to lend support to Musa Anter. A group of 49 mainly young Kurds supported Anter. They were immediately detained, accused of 'participating in activities aimed at separating the unity of the state and parts of the territory of the state'. This now famous '49ers Case' was part of a plan of the Turkish government to prosecute thousands of Kurdish activists for crimes carrying the death penalty. The aim was to suppress rising Kurdish nationalism in the region, centred among others on the legendary Kurdish leader Mustafa Barzani, who had in 1958 returned to Iraq from exile in the Soviet Union, and who had launched his revolt against Baghdad. None of the group was in the end sentenced to death, owing partly to an amnesty – but the scene was set for Musa Anter's political and cultural life.

In total Anter spent almost 12 years of his life in various prisons. He wrote books, columns, poems and articles for many newspapers and magazines, including the largest Kurdish newspaper, Özgür Gündem, right up to his death. He was also involved in setting up a number of Kurdish organisations that were extremely important for the Kurdish political movement, such as the Revolutionary Eastern Cultural Hearths, the Mesopotamia Cultural Centre, the Workers' Party of the People and the Kurdish Institute in Istanbul.

On 20 September 1992 – he was by now 72 – he spent the day signing his books at an arts and culture festival in Diyarbakir, the largest Kurdish city in the south-east of Turkey. In the evening he received a phone call asking him whether he would help in resolving a land dispute. He and his family member and fellow activist Orhan Miroglu were picked up at their hotel. Anter and Miroglu were subsequently shot in an outer suburb of the city – Miroglu only just survived.

Anter's son Dicle, the youngest of his three children, had this explanation for his father's murder on the news portal bianet.org: 'Many people were irritated by my father's visions. Because, despite the fact that he spent years in prison and despite being tortured on many occasions, he has resisted all his life. I believe that is the reason a decision was taken to eliminate him.'

Musa Anter's murder has never been solved.

CHAPTER 5

SELF-REGULATION

What all news media in Turkey have in common, however, whether they are financially independent of the government or not, is that they decidedly choose sides in the political spectrum and pursue campaign-like journalism of varying quality.

This goes, however, beyond the 'signature' that newspapers and TV stations virtually always have, defined as a political or ideological view of the world that determines the spectacles through which they watch and interpret the news. The UK has the left-wing Guardian, and The Times, a daily that is rather more to the right of centre. In France there is Le Figaro on the right of the political spectrum, Le Monde more to the left, and La Croix leftist with a Catholic background. In Germany the conservative-liberal Frankfurter Allgemeine Zeitung, the liberal weekly Die Zeit and more to the left of centre the Süddeutsche Zeitung. The Netherlands has the Volkskrant left of centre, NRC right-wing-liberal, Trouw with a religious slant.

But this sort of signature does not have to get in the way of professional journalism. Journalists uphold generally accepted journalistic rules, and there is an ethical code that journalists should abide by. The core of this package of practical and ethical rules is that it is your task as journalist to seek the truth, that you write up what occurred or show it as it happened.

In certain cases this is fairly simple: a journalist who observes a road accident after a driver goes through a red light is able to write up an account of the facts fairly easily. If the reporter arrives on the scene only later, it gets more difficult and he or she has to hope that the police will provide information and or speak to witnesses and assess their reliability. In times of war things become even more problematic: as a war reporter you may well see that there is shooting, or that a home is hit, but where did the firing come from? There are of course ways of finding out: from which direction did the firing come and which group has that area under their control? What kinds of munitions were used, and which of the parties to the conflict has access to them? Whichever side in the fighting you ask, they will all probably give you a different answer, and independent sources are often difficult to find. Who do you quote, and why? What are the facts? However difficult the facts might be to find on occasion, as a journalist you are always looking for them. And if you do not know the facts, and if they cannot be reconstructed, you say so and quote your sources, who may be able to throw light on the matter, along with their role and any feelings of support for the sides in the conflict – or whatever your article is about. Stories where the truth is difficult or impossible to ascertain always benefit from an independent expert outsider, for example an observer from an organisation not party to the conflict, or an academic. Journalists themselves may also function as independent outsiders, if they have gone into a subject thoroughly and have themselves become specialists. Another important rule is listening to both sides, which means that you grant someone the right to relate their version of an event if they are accused of something. A journalist who discovers that politician A. has tampered with funding will gather as much evidence as possible, then make contact with the politician to present the allegations and to ask for comment. Rebel movement X stands accused of deploying child soldiers and gets the opportunity to react to this accusation before the story goes to print, can be watched on TV or is published online.

Then there is the hotly debated question of objectivity: a journalist is supposed to describe objectively what happens and to maintain objectivity at all times. But there is no such thing as objectivity. Choices are always made, and those choices are made not by machines but by people, and in addition a news medium's signature plays a role. A newspaper with an extensive network of correspondents all over the world reveals the significance it attaches to foreign affairs, a newspaper with a reporter in the Vatican shows that it regards following the Roman Catholic Church closely as important. One regional broadcaster chooses to report on a particular crossing that is not safe for cyclists, while another does not. Moreover it depends on the journalistic genre whether an article has to, or can be, purely objective or not. To stick with the example of a road accident, you write up precisely what happened when and where, who was involved and why it happened. You leave out your own opinions and non-factual observations: the girl was not riding an 'ugly' bicycle, and the motorist was not driving a 'macho car'.

With a backgrounder the main thing is balance, and you usually show several sides of a story, for example if it is an article on discrimination in the labour market. You not only allow victims and researchers to tell their side of the story, but you also allow employers to speak about the value they attach to a varied staff complement and how they themselves try to prevent discrimination in interview procedures – if they do. Here too you seek the truth. If there are various investigations that show that discrimination in the labour market is on the rise, you do not write a story on how things are going well, unless it emerges from your own thorough investigation that there are things to criticise about the investigations.

Your perspective is determined by your signature and what you as a journalist find important. A financial and business newspaper will prefer to reflect the employer's perspective, the Muslim broadcaster interviews Muslim youth on their experiences, a mainstream newspaper paints a more general picture. Subjective choices, but they can still provide a balanced article that does not violate the truth. But if the financial and business newspaper describes employers as champions of non-discrimination, they are being disingenuous, and if the Muslim broadcaster makes out that no Muslim is able to find a job in the Netherlands, the editors are being dishonest.

Then there are the genres that are subjective by definition: reviews, opinion pieces, editorials, columns. The column is the freest form, in which you as columnist are able to disregard journalistic rules: you may exaggerate, invent events, conjure up non-existent people – it does not matter. That emphatically does not apply to the other genres. A reviewer does not pan a book or concert without argument, an opinion piece is ideally based on facts and deploys argument in order to convince, an editorial must reveal knowledge of the topic and not just shoot from the hip. These are genres intended to advance opinions, to provoke debate, to evoke anger or by contrast agreement, to stimulate readers' thoughts and to shake up their viewpoint.

_ Editorial content and commercial interests

Erosion of journalistic rules and ethics is always a danger. Is a newspaper free to print that instead of drinking mineral water you can just as well drink straight from the tap if the parent company of the mineral water producer is the largest advertiser in the newspaper? Can a US commercial channel be strongly critical of a presidential candidate who enjoys the support of a company that places adverts with that broadcaster?
The so-called 'editorial code of conduct' has been created for all these situations, a document that lays down the independence of the editorial staff of a newspaper, magazine or TV programme. It sets out the journalistic nature of the news medium, lays down ethical rules for journalism and regulates the strict separation of editorial content and commercial interests.

In conclusion there is also an indispensable rule that politicians must allow the press to operate properly and freely: they do not interfere in the media. The prime minister does not criticise a revelation in the newspaper that causes him difficulty, the justice minister does not lay down the developments that a newspaper or TV programme has to report on, the president does not lash out at journalists who repeatedly scrutinise his actions, nor does he call on people not to read certain newspapers because he considers them 'traitors'.

Of course, these rules and guarantees do not function flawlessly, of course there is ongoing discussion on choices of stories and on how these stories are approached, of course mistakes are made and stories appear in the newspaper where the journalist went completely wrong or even dreamed up events and quotes deliberately, and these mistakes are sometimes serious and damaging. But then it is important that the media regulate themselves, that journalists who invent stories are fired and that the underlying editorial structures are held up to the light to prevent fabricated stories or reports appearing again in the newspaper or on TV. That there is ongoing discussion within the profession on why and how certain issues are reported on. That those feeling themselves placed at a disadvantage by an article or item somewhere in the media can have their grievances heard, and the journalistic product is evaluated according to the professional standards. That in the final instance the courts can decide whether laws have been broken through journalistic work, for example the laws governing slander and libel.

This self-regulating mechanism is essential for the media organisations that take themselves seriously. Credibility is their main capital. If they use it up and their reporting is no longer taken seriously, they are undermining their own right to exist. This also applies to individual journalists. Anyone failing to observe the rules of journalism can forget their career. Like Jayson Blair, after it emerged in 2003 that he had on occasion plagiarised stories for the New York Times and had invented facts. He's out, and he will never work in the profession again.

_ Shrug shoulders

Back to Turkey, to the capital Ankara, and the offices of the major newspaper Hürriyet. 'Our Basic Principles' are up on the wall leading to the newsroom, the twenty rules that the newspaper's journalists have to uphold. One reads: 'The basic function of journalism is to inform the public as quickly as possible about the truth, without violating the truth by changing or exaggerating it.' That is the way it should be. But Hürriyet often fails to uphold this.

An incident from 2011 is indicative, when the newspaper wrote sensationally about Serzh Sargsyan, the president of Armenia, who was reported to have called, in a speech on the youth of his country, for the

85

reconquest of 'Western Armenia', a geographic reference that everyone in Armenia and Turkey knows refers to eastern Turkey. The fear of losing land to Armenia is one of the reasons why Turkey can still not bring itself to acknowledge the Armenian genocide, and there was outrage at this threat to Turkey's national integrity. Many newspapers and TV stations picked up the Hürriyet reporting, and politicians, including Prime Minister Erdogan, were jumping up and down in anger. However, it was not true. Hürriyet had twisted the words of the Armenian president. The newspaper admitted this later, but by then the damage had been done.

Did the senior editors resign? Was the journalist or the news editor who twisted the words fired? And did heads roll at the other newspapers and TV broadcasters that picked up the story without checking it themselves? Nothing of the kind. Shrug your shoulders and get on with tomorrow's newspaper. Nor did the readers react with indignation to deliberately false reporting of this kind by newspapers. On the contrary, stories like these are lapped up. The average Turk is happy to hear anti-Armenian sentiment, and if they read that the Armenian president did not incite young people to seize Turkish territory, they would rather believe that that is the lie.

There is absolutely no self-regulatory mechanism for the Turkish press. And that situation arises largely because providing journalistic work is not the aim of most of the Turkish media. They do not regard seeking and unravelling the truth as their most important task. How then should you address them about trampling underfoot the rules of the journalist's profession? In order to sell as many newspapers as possible and to score the highest possible viewing figures with the aim of humouring the government and boosting the profits of the parent company, the aim is to spice the news with the polarisation, sensation, sex, sexism and nationalism that the average Turk enjoys, if possible with a good dose of anti-Armenian, anti-Kurdish and anti-Semitic feeling added in. Truth? Who cares?

And this applies emphatically not only to those media that are part of large companies, but also to some of the independent newspapers.

Different journalistic genres that are always strictly separated in the quality media are cheerfully mixed up in many Turkish newspapers. News reports that should be factual are embellished with shrieking opinion, the principle that you should give someone you have accused of something the opportunity to defend themselves is seldom if ever observed (and the allegations are often fabricated and rarely backed up with facts), balanced background stories in which several viewpoints from different people involved are offered and views are supported with facts and argument are rarely to be found even if you look for them.

And more: rumours are frequently printed as fact, and the complete lie has for years been gaining ground, especially in the media directly linked to the government.

For example, the Takvim editorial staff are crazy about manipulating photographs. In the summer of 2015, this 'newspaper' printed a front page story about a young woman who was abducted and drugged by the PKK, and even had a belt loaded with explosives strapped around her by the armed group. There was a photograph of the woman, with in fact an explosives belt around her middle and in the company of PKK fighters. But the real photograph soon turned up.

The woman had been travelling by bus in the east of Turkey, where she had to alight at a PKK roadblock, along with all the other passengers. The PKK blocks roads in this way regularly in order to underline its power and presence in those parts of the country. They check the travellers' identity documents and give a lecture in PKK ideology, after which the travellers can go on their way. On the original, genuine photograph the young woman was standing in a line in front of the bus with other passengers and a couple of PKK fighters standing around them. Takvim started Photoshopping: the editorial team cut the woman and a PKK member out of the photograph, stuck the pair in a remote landscape with a few other fighters around them, Photoshopped an explosives belt around her waist and stuck it on the front page. It emerged later that the woman had got into serious difficulty as a result of the report. She was recognised and people in the town where she lived suspected her of PKK sympathies.

Takvim's readership believes a story like this because it fits exactly into their worldview, and the actual photograph and the manipulation behind it never reach them, because they do not read newspapers other than those the government likes to put in front of them. The manipulation is writ large on social media, but Twitter is not that big in Turkey, certainly not among ordinary Turks or in an average Anatolian city. Facebook, which is very big in Turkey, is in general used primarily for private purposes. And even if the true story were to reach Takvim readers, they would not believe it.

How can you put out a genuine quality newspaper in a climate like this? How can you as a newspaper resist the slander and hate that come your way if you publish a story exposing the government? If you as the bearer of news are verbally lynched by the country's most powerful people? As Can Dündar said in the interview in Chapter 1: 'Once a society is as polarised as Turkey is at the moment, your readers expect you to take a stand. Nobody wants the media to be calm and objective anymore.'
During the interview Dündar held up the front page of the Cumhuriyet of 2 June 2015 showing photographs of the newspaper's editors with their signatures, with the headline 'I am responsible'. The journalists were reacting to President Erdogan, who had made clear that those responsible for revealing the MIT weapons transports would pay a high price. Solidarity certainly, but is it journalism? 'I hate it,' Dündar sighed, shaking his head at the sight of the front page concerned. 'We see this as a war'.

_ If trust is lacking
Taking up positions is a logical consequence of the fact that the press functions badly and of the increasingly intense polarisation in Turkey. Those who feel they are systematically ignored by the mainstream newspapers and TV channels, who day in and day out see that the stories in the media have nothing to do with the reality around them, ultimately set up their own newspaper or TV channel with like-minded people.

The danger is of course that it becomes increasingly more difficult to
see the world through another's eyes. Not only because you are keen to
disseminate your view of the news and current affairs, but also because
people outside your own circle often no longer want to talk to you for
articles, just as the AKP government no longer speaks to Cumhuriyet. I saw
that myself after being detained and in the run-up to my court case at the
start of 2015: Today's Zaman, a Gülen movement newspaper, asked me for
an interview, but I absolutely refused, fearing that a newspaper supporting
the prosecution of Kurdish journalists would depict me as a propagandist
for terrorism. They might possibly not have done so – we will never know
– but if trust is lacking in a situation that is in any case stressful, there is
nothing more to be said.

In that light it was kind of Bülent Kenes, editor of Today's Zaman from
2007 to December 2015, to grant my request for an interview. And also to
speak about a much-debated issue from the newspaper's past: the support
of the Gülen movement, which the movement itself prefers to call the
'Hizmet' movement, referring to the call of its supporters to provide hizmet,
service, to society, for two court cases going back over the past 10 years.
One of the cases was about 'Ergekenon', a suspected planned coup by
senior military officers that was revealed by the Taraf daily in 2008. It
was soon clear that some of the evidence had been tampered with and
that certain items of evidence had even been fabricated, but the Gülen
media continued to support and defend the trial, along with the arrest
of journalists said to have been involved in the coup plans in one way or
another. One of the journalists was Ahmet Sik, an investigative journalist
who wrote a critical book on the Gülen movement and was detained before
the book was published. Another was Soner Yalcin, a columnist at OdaTV,
a website that has always been critical of Erdogan and was reported to
have been ready to assist the officers allegedly carrying out the coup by
justifying it with articles and columns – allegations for which no evidence
has ever been found.

Another was the KCK case, a trial that started in the spring of 2009, for which hundreds of politically active Kurds were detained, including mayors and other local officials, members of parliament, lawyers, human rights activists, journalists and activists. The KCK, the Group of Communities in Kurdistan, is a Kurdish umbrella organisation that the armed PKK is part of. Not one of those accused had ever taken up arms against the state but they had in fact used democratic means to fight for change in Turkey. This political case was also defended by the Gülen media, including locking up around 40 journalists on charges of terrorism.

How does Kenes look back on the past and his support for the prosecution of journalists?

The former editor explains firstly that his newspaper sees the KCK as a terrorist organisation that the PKK is part of, and which is thus responsible for terrorist attacks, and so it supported operations against the KCK. The Ergenekon court case was also supported because the newspaper found that the army's authority was in the way of Turkey's democratisation and its future membership of the EU. 'We always thought that legal investigations of this kind were opportunities for the democratisation of Turkey.'

He goes on: 'However, looking back I see that we did not notice certain violations of rights and for that reason failed to criticise them sufficiently. It was not deliberate, but we were unable to be sufficiently sensitive to these violations in the heat of the struggle for more democracy.' However, he expresses virulent opposition to the suggestion that Today's Zaman became critical of the AKP government only after the December 2013 corruption scandal. Kenes: 'For example, in 2005 we spoke out against amendments to the counter-terrorism legislation that made it possible to prosecute people for terrorism even if they had not used arms, and to the effect that a 'terrorist organisation' could in future consist of a single person. We also wrote critically about the AKP on other topics. We have always stood on the side of freedom and democracy.'

What irritates him is the perception on the part of outsiders that all the media linked to the Gülen movement have the same editorial policy: 'Today's Zaman is not an English language copy of Zaman; we have a separate newsroom and largely different columnists. The TV broadcasters of the Hizmet movement all have their own editorial teams. You can't gauge us on the basis of articles and columns in other media.'

After all, columnists on the same newspaper do not always have the same opinion. Where certain Zaman columnists did back locking up journalists like Ahmet Sik, who was prosecuted for his book of revelations on the Hizmet movement and for being in the 'media arm' of Ergenekon, Bülent Kenes says that this support was not general policy at the newspaper: 'We would never defend arresting journalists. Today's Zaman itself has published articles in which holding Ahmet Sik and others on remand was criticised.'

To the question of whether he has started to think differently on press freedom over recent years, he says: 'Naturally, as a result of the pressure from the takeover of TV channels and radio stations close to the Hizmet movement and of the police raids on the offices of Zaman and Today's Zaman and the arrest of staff, we have begun to better grasp the importance of press freedom and freedom of expression. Sensitivity for violations of rights of this kind has improved. But that does not mean that the news media close to the Hizmet movement were previously insensitive to the importance of press freedom and freedom of expression. So, although there is no reason for far-reaching change in how we deal with these issues, we can definitely say that the anti-democratic pressure being exerted on the free media of the Hizmet movement has taken sensitivity to a new plane.'

_ Journalism as quest for truth
It would not be that bad if the press did not have a crucial role in the democratic process. If the most important job of the press was not

informing ordinary people as well as possible and putting politicians, policy makers and other powerful actors – such as businesses – constantly under a critical spotlight, so that people are able to make informed choices on how they arrange their lives and who they want to administer and rule them at local and national level.

Lack of press freedom and qualitatively good journalism and a lack of democracy have each other in a stranglehold. Without press freedom and without a qualitatively good press, no democracy, and without democracy no press freedom and qualitatively high-level journalism. Things could not have gone as wrong in Turkey as they now have if there had not been structural flaws in the fabric of the system. The ruling AKP and former Prime Minister, now President, Erdogan could not have dragged down the level of democracy, press freedom and the quality of the press as far as he has, if Turkey had had a firm democratic base with a tradition of journalism for journalism's sake, with a history of journalism as a quest for the truth and nothing else.

The average Turkish citizen is left with the consequences. For them it is extremely difficult to find out what is actually going on in the country. Add to that the increasing polarisation, and the situation is getting further out of hand. Many Turks have taken up their positions and no longer want to know what is really going on, because they assume in advance that information from the opposite side is wrong by definition.

The love for Erdogan is absolute, the hatred of Erdogan is absolute. Turkey was polarised in previous decades, but much less so than now. The years of AKP rule have also ensured that a large group of Turks, which was virtually invisible previously and had no or scarcely any political or economic power, is now a power factor of significance: the conservative Islamic population in the towns and villages of Anatolia. They form the AKP's grassroots support, and they are grateful and loyal to the party because the AKP, and Erdogan in particular, have given them a significant position in society. Previously the 'secular' elite held the power in politics and the economy. Their newly acquired power has pushed the old elite into second place, and they are resisting.

But there is also an increasingly large group of Turks who do not feel at home in either group. These are often young, urban, usually better educated and modern Turks who feel that there is no place for them in Erdogan's Turkey. These were the people who objected in 2013 to the disappearance of Gezi Park in Istanbul, who demonstrated on a grand scale against the AKP government when their protests were ruthlessly suppressed. The protests may have died down, but the dissatisfaction remains, because Erdogan has changed nothing in his type of democracy in which the majority decides and the minority has to put up with it – on the contrary. Add the powder keg of the Kurdish issue, which has exploded again with full force since mid 2015, and the contradictions are complete.

Among those facing the consequences are the reporters who earn their living in this journalistic climate, who write the news stories in the newsrooms, who get the stories with mud on their feet. In the many conversations that the author had with these reporters over recent years, a large degree of frustration came to the surface. A news editor at a major 'mainstream' newspaper in answer to the question why her newspaper never asked ordinary Kurds about their lives or opinions: 'There's no point, because we can't write it up anyway.'

Apart from the fact that Turkish journalism does in general not give 'ordinary Turks' the chance to voice their opinions on the news and how it impacts on their lives, the answer was indicative. Reporters going onto the street or into the countryside to track down stories, news editors checking national and international sources of news the whole day, are unable to divulge through their media what they know and discover. If you do not provide stories that fit into the framework that the editor demands, in other words if you fail to provide stories that do not cause your senior manager trouble with the authorities in Ankara, you will be put out onto the street.

And because the real stories do not come out anyway, scraping them together becomes increasingly difficult. To illustrate this, a few conversations that the author had with Turkish journalists at the end of 2014 certainly clarify this. The battle for Kobani, the Syrian Kurdish city that was held by the Kurds but was attacked by ISIS, was raging. Kobani lies close to the border with Turkey, and on the other side of the border there is a hill with a good view of the town. You heard from a distance the US F16s that were supporting the Kurds, and a little later you heard the bombs falling and saw the plumes of smoke rising where they had hit their targets. It was to the west of the city or to the south.

Many members of the national and international press had gathered on this 'press hill', which was accessible only with a press card. The writer of this book was there only occasionally. Kurds from all over Turkey streamed into the villages close to the Turkish side of the border to support the Kurdish fighters in Kobani with singing, dancing, banners and human chains. Those were lovely, hopeful stories. And the battle between the Kurds on the Turkish side of the border and the Turkish security services and border control could be followed easily in the villages. Kurdish demonstrators attempted to get as close as possible to the border to make known their support for Kobani, and sometimes groups of youths tried to break through the border to take up arms against ISIS. 'Why are you standing around here all the time?' I asked the Turkish journalists on presshill. 'There in the villages is where the stories on what's going on here are taking place.' One of the TV journalists said: 'We know that. But for one thing, our station will not broadcast those stories anyway. And for another, the people in those villages will not talk to us, because they don't trust our station. And they are right.'

ÇETIN EMEÇ (1935-1990)

Emeç was just 25 when he was appointed in 1960 to manage the newspaper Son Posta. This was the year that Turkey saw its first military coup. The young Çetin took over the position at the newspaper from his father after he was detained on account of his political activities for the Democratic Party of Prime Minister Adnan Menderes, which he had helped to found.

Emeç started his career as a journalist in 1952, while he was studying law at the University of Istanbul. He was editor of the popular monthlies Hayat (Life) and Ses (Voice) until 1972. He then made a career at the major national newspapers Hürriyet and Milliyet, as news editor, director and columnist of note.

On 7 March 1990 he had just got into his car to go to work, when two masked gunmen opened fire through the rear doors. Emeç's chauffeur Sinan Ercan, who attempted to flee, died immediately. Emeç was taken to hospital with seven gunshot wounds, but was dead on arrival. Two organisations claimed responsibility on the day of the murder. One was the Union of Turkish-Islamic Commandos, a militant group from Iran that phoned the newspaper to announce that they intended to murder everyone working at Hürriyet. The other was Dev-Sol (Revolutionary Left), the precursor of the DHKP-C (Revolutionary National Liberation Party Front), a Marxist-Leninist group that is still active. Who in fact has the murder on their conscience and who gave the orders has never been cleared up, just as there is no clarity on the motive for the murder.

Çetin Emeç lies buried in Istanbuİs Zincirliköyü Cemetery. Roads and streets in a number of Turkish cities have been named after him, as well as a football stadium in Istanbul. Emeç was married with a daughter and a son.

ABDI IPEKCI (1929-1979)

Abdi Ipekci had been editor of Milliyet, at the time a newspaper of the moderate left, when he was shot and killed in Istanbul in 1979. He had just arrived by car at the apartment block where he lived, at the end of the working day. In Abdi Ipekci, Turkey did not only lose a respected editor, journalist and intellectual, but also a human rights activist, an advocate of better relations with Greece – at the time seen as a major enemy after the 1974 Cyprus crisis – and an opponent of political extremism. The latter was highly significant in those days, as at the end of the 1970s political violence was out of hand in Turkey. Extremists on the right and left murdered each other in public in broad daylight, and competing leftist groups were engaged in deadly feuds. With at times up to 10 political murders a day, the total number killed rose to around 5,000 in the second half of the 1970s. Abdi Ipekci was one of the victims of this wave of violence.

His killers, Oral Çelik and Mehmet Ali Agca, turned out to be members of the Grey Wolves, the youth wing of the ultra-nationalist MHP party, one of the murderous groups on the streets at the time. Mehmet Ali Agca was arrested and sentenced to life in prison. However, he spent just six months in jail before escaping from Istanbul's military prison with the help of military officials and the Grey Wolves. He fled initially to Iran, from where he went to Bulgaria, at the time a Turkish mafia hotbed. In May 1981 he carried out an attack on Pope John Paul II in the Vatican.

Abdi Ipekci was born into a well-to-do Istanbul family in 1929. He studied law for a time, but was then drawn to journalism, beginning his career as a sports journalist. When he joined Milliyet in 1954, he immediately took over the day-to-day running of the newspaper and was appointed editor in 1959. In addition, he was active in the Turkish Union of Journalists, the Turkish Press Institute, the Istanbul section of the Journalists Association and the International Press Institute.

Ipekci's murder was not a spontaneous street killing, but rather a conspiracy planned to the last detail. The Grey Wolf Mehmet Ali Agca was the perpetrator, claiming initially that he had acted alone. But later he revealed a whole list of names of people who planned the murder and organised the weapon. Two of them, Mehmet Sener and Yalcin Özbey, fled abroad. Özbey turned up in Germany, which turned down Turkey's application for extradition. Sener has never been arrested. Another plotter, Yavuz Caylan, received a 10-year jail sentence.

Finally Agca provided the name of one of the most important people behind the murder – Oral Çelik. Although he has spent a number of years in prison in different European countries for drug smuggling and other crimes, he has never been prosecuted or even interrogated regarding his involvement in Ipekci's murder, despite the fact that he returned to Turkey voluntarily. He was released after being held for three months.

Abdi Ipekci left his widow, Sibel, a daughter, Nükhet, and a son, Sedat. The street where he lived is now called Abdi Ipekci Avenue, and there has been a bronze statute commemorating him in Istanbul since 2000. In 2000 the International Press Institute named him one of the 50 World Press Freedom Heroes of the past 50 years.

CHAPTER 6

HOPE

There is no hope of structural improvement in the situation of the news media in Turkey. The constitution will probably be changed within the foreseeable future, but not in a way that does justice to Turkey's pluralist society and that protects the citizen against state meddling. On the contrary: it is in the interest of President Erdogan and the ruling AKP to further centralise power in Ankara and to replace parliamentary democracy with a presidential system. This book provides an outline of what that means in a country in which strong political leaders are demigods and there are scarcely any independent institutions left, such as the courts, that are able to enforce the observance of democratic values, including press freedom.

For the time being there will also be no end to the problems associated with the ownership of many newspapers and TV stations in Turkey, simply because no one with even a modicum of power in the Turkish media world wants this. Not the super rich media magnates, not the well paid columnists at mainstream media and government newspapers, not the government. It works too well, that is to say lucratively, for too many people who do not care a fig for journalism or democracy.

And those to whom it does matter – some journalists in reporting, the journalist association and trade unions, certain opposition politicians and some academics and intellectuals, and a growing group of concerned citizens – simply do not have enough power to change the situation for the better.

The EU? Shouldn't it be able to set stringent requirements in renewed accession talks with Turkey? It should be able to do this. But European government leaders are more frightened of Erdogan's threat to open its borders with Greece and Bulgaria to the 2.5 million Syrian refugees in his country who want to travel to Europe than they are really worried about the continued eradication of the few traces of democracy that still exist in Turkey.

Nevertheless I conclude my book with hope. It is to be found in the current situation, strangely enough. Turkey is bursting with initiatives aiming to give a boost to journalism, and there are journalists who love their profession sufficiently to take big and sometimes personal risks.

I interviewed three initiators and persistent stayers. Firstly Erdal Güven, editor of Diken.com.tr (Thorn), a news website that went online at the beginning of 2014 and puts out the news in an independent, tireless and critical way. I interviewed Güven at the Diken offices in Istanbul in August 2015.

Secondly Engin Önder, initiator of the Twitter account @140journos, which put out its first tweets in January 2012. For as many as 93,000 followers, @140journos has become essential for keeping abreast of events in Turkey. I interviewed Önder via Skype in February 2016.

Thirdly: Haci Bogatekin, a self-employed journalist in the town of Gerger in the south-eastern province of Adiyaman. It could be seen as a miracle that Bogatekin's local newspaper, Gerger Firat, first published on 10 July 1992, still exists. If it had been up to the local and provincial authorities and courts, Bogatekin would long since have thrown in the towel. But he does not even consider giving up. In December 2015 I mailed the founder and editor a list of questions, which he answered quickly and expansively.

These are three examples, but of course there are more. I would like to select two. Firstly the independent online news provider T24, set up by, among others, former Taraf deputy editor Yasemin Congar. An old hand in the profession, Hasan Cemal, a journalist for 45 years, also writes for T24. He ended up there after writing up in Milliyet, the newspaper that he had worked at for 15 years, notes of conversations between PKK leader Öcalan and a delegation of HDP MPs who visited him in the context of peace talks. Then Prime Minister Erdogan was furious at this scoop and thundered in public that the principle of press freedom did not give the media the right to act against the interests of the state, saying to Cemal in addition: 'Down with your journalism, if this is the journalism you will conduct!' Cemal was eventually forced to resign from Milliyet. T24 is independent, uncensored and critical, and moreover has a number of lawyers associated with it to advise their journalist colleagues and support them legally.

Apart from that, there are innumerable websites putting out more or less independent news, often run by individuals or mini-teams that closely cover their own district or province and also publish national news. They too represent hope, if only because they are enthusiastic about sending uncensored stories into the world.

Secondly, the brand new initiative 'Haber Nöbeti' (news service), created at the beginning of February 2016. Teams of journalists from the west of Turkey travel for a week to the Kurdish south-east to assist their fellow journalists there in reporting the news. Since the ceasefire between the armed Kurdish PKK and the Turkish state broke down in the summer of 2015 violence has soared in the south-east, and Kurdish journalists are once more under enormous pressure. Reporters from Kurdish media, such as the Dicle and Jinha news agencies and the newspapers Özgür Gündem and Azadiya Welat are being detained or (fatally) wounded almost daily as a result of the violence. Freelance journalists work for Haber Nöbeti along with reporters from small and independent newspapers, websites and radio stations, such as Agos, Evrensel, Bianet.org, BirGün, Acik Radyo, T24, P24, Diken and Cumhuriyet. Those 'on duty' send in their reports via the Twitter account @haber_nobeti and through their own media.

_ **Erdal Güven, editor of Diken: 'I'm obsessed with quality journalism'**
Erdal Güven, editor and co-founder of the journalistic website Diken.com. tr (Thorn), regrets the fact that he did not resign from his last permanent job immediately after a new editor-in-chief was appointed in 2010. That was at Radikal, a small newspaper from the Dogan stable, where Güven

started in the foreign news department in 1996 and later became news editor. He recalls with astonishment how certain stories suddenly had to be covered. For example there was a story about a young woman, a student, who was kicked by a police officer during a demonstration against Erdogan and lost her unborn baby as a result. 'The new editor did not want to make a big story out of it, although the woman had lost her baby,' Güven says. 'How could it not be a big story? A little later the book by the journalist Ahmet Sik came out, a book about the Gülen movement. Ahmet Sik was detained, and I found the way in which we reported on it contributed to criminalising Sik's journalistic work. As if it were normal to prosecute a journalist! I believed we should criticise it strongly, but we didn't do that.'

Radikal, a newspaper that is currently published only online, was at the time making the transition from broadsheet to tabloid, and Güven felt that because of that he could not simply leave. Once he had decided to go, he did not give voice to his thoughts until he made sure he got his remuneration, and then he was gone. 'Radikal was not completely free under the previous editor-in-chief, but we were a small newspaper and had greater freedom of movement because our headlines did not have as much impact as those of Hürriyet for example,' says Güven. 'We always took that position to the limits. But once there was a new editor-in-chief, we were never again reined in by the management. That says it all.'

Erdal Güven is sitting on Diken's spacious balcony on the top floor of a building in the heart of Istanbul. The offices will soon move to cheaper premises, as the rent is rising sharply and Diken has a chronic shortage of money. 'Working for Diken is incredibly satisfying professionally and spiritually, but one thing hurts: our finances are insufficient to take on more people,' he says. 'If we had two or three more editors and two or three good reporters, we would be able to grow, have more visitors and be known and respected.'

Diken was set up in January 2014. It was the winter following the 2013 Gezi protests, which Güven covered along with a friend who had also worked at Dogan as a journalist, Harun Simavi. 'We sat drinking raki and dreaming out loud about journalism. He had some money and said that he wanted to devote it to journalism.[4] We knew that there was an opening for a journalistic medium that could be critical without being hampered by the owner's demands.'

Simavi and Güven discussed it for a couple of months, cut through the knot and secured the domain name diken.com.tr. Güven: 'My sole condition was that there would be no censorship and no restrictions on the content at all, by any outsider whatsoever. We alone would decide what to write, and no one else.' He compares what he envisaged with a small boutique hotel: 'A cool, attractive and high-quality address, not impersonal five-star luxury accommodation.'

Diken publishes its own news with a few freelancers, has a number of columnists (including the well known Amberin Zaman and Hayko Bagdat, who previously wrote for Taraf) and puts out the news from other sources from a critical Diken perspective. Güven: 'And in this we always stick to the journalistic rules. If Prime Minister Davutoglu makes a speech, we will quote from it without violating his words, although we will add critical remarks. This is how we create our own tone.' Diken now has around seven million unique visitors per month.

The author of this book, who had a column at Diken from January 2014 till her expulsion from Turkey in September 2015, has in fact never experienced censorship from Diken, not even in columns expressing sharp opinions. There is respect for all opinions, and columns from other newspapers, including those of the government newspapers, are quoted. In this way the Diken reader acquires a good picture of the news and also of the opinions about that news. This is unique, because you would normally have to read a whole bunch of newspapers before you are up-to-

---

4 Harun Simavi is the grandson of Sedat Simavi, founder of the Turkish Journalists Association (1946) and daily Hürriyet (1948). Sedat Simavi worked as journalist, fiction and non-fiction writer, cartoonist and film director.

date on the opinions of the various extremes in Turkish society. Nevertheless, Güven did remove a publication from the internet in order to avoid problems. This concerned the famous 'Mohammed cover' of the French satirical magazine Charlie Hebdo, in January 2015. Güven: 'We published the cover. The daily Cumhuriyet also published it, as did the independent portal T24. A dangerous situation arose at Cumhuriyet, where there were demonstrations in front of the building and threats were received. The public prosecutor opened an investigation into two Cumhuriyet journalists regarding the cartoons, and T24 was asked to remove them. We were not asked to do anything, but I was worried. I thought about what would happen if a few of these angry men turned up at the Diken offices. How would we be able to defend ourselves? The reality is that we wouldn't be able to. We do not have any security here the way Cumhuriyet does. We are so vulnerable. The Mohammed cover had been online for two days and was no longer in the top10 of our most visited pages. I took it offline.' Güven sighs showing his hands and looking at them: 'With my own hands.'

There are other Diken pages that cannot be accessed, but only because they have been censored by the courts. Access to around 10 pages has been blocked as the contents are supposed to be prohibited. They are primarily about a prosecutor being held hostage in the Caglayan courthouse in Istanbul, in March 2015. The prosecutor was held at gunpoint by two hostage takers of the extreme leftist DHKP-C, who said they had targeted the prosecutor because he had blocked the investigation into the death of Berkin Elvan, a 15-year-old boy who went out to buy bread during the Gezi protests in 2013 and was hit by a police teargas grenade, later dying of head wounds. Police negotiated for hours with the hostage takers, but went in after hearing gunshots and shot them. The prosecutor did not survive his wounds after being shot by the hostage takers. Publication of a photograph of the prosecutor with a pistol to his temple was immediately banned by the authorities, it was said to be terrorist propaganda, and the news about it generated a few Diken links that no longer work.

There is a legal inquiry into Diken concerning an article on the attacks in the border town of Suruc in July 2015. Thirty-three people were killed there as they were about to travel to Kobani on the other side of the border in Syria, with the aim of helping to rebuild the city after the battle between Kurdish troops and ISIS attackers between September 2014 and January 2015. Güven: 'We published an opinion piece in which we queried how it was that the Anadolu state news agency was on the scene so unbelievably soon after the attack. But I really won't take a story of that kind offline. Let the court cases roll. I'm not afraid of the authorities, but I do fear the maniacs as in the case of the Charlie Hebdo cartoons.'

If you are prepared to make sacrifices, you can still be a good and critical journalist, Erdal Güven believes. If only more money could be earned from it. 'I'm not in this to make money, but we need it to invest in journalists and to improve our quality. I'm obsessed by quality journalism.'

_ **Engin Önder of @140journos: 'Our reputation must not be harmed'**
'All journalists out!' the judge ruled. It was 21 January 2012 in the Caglayan courthouse in Istanbul, where the first session in the well known OdaTV case was being held. Journalist Soner Yalcin of OdaTV, an ultranationalist website strongly opposed to the government that was set up in 2007, stood accused along with his website of being the 'media arm' of Ergekenon, the alleged conspiracy of top-level military officers aimed at toppling the AKP government (see Chapter 5). The judge disapproved of the way that journalists in the public gallery were tweeting details on the case, and so all journalists had to leave the courtroom.
Engin Önder: 'I was allowed to remain because I did not have a press card. We had just launched our Twitter account @140journos and had around 100 followers. The journalists who had been excluded soon realised that @140journos was still tweeting from inside the courtroom. They followed us, re-tweeting our material. By the end of the day we had more than 1,000 followers.'

More than four years later @140journos is fast approaching 100,000 followers, with an unshakeable reputation as an account that puts out only news that has been checked. All things considered, if @140journos tweets it, it has happened. "Only the facts' was our format from the first day,' says co-founder Engin Önder. 'The idea was born after the bombing of Roboski on 28 December 2011 (see chapter 2), and the way in which the press dealt with it. The news media were used as an instrument to contribute to the polarisation in Turkey, and we wanted to counter this with something. Facts, and leave the comment to others.'

The first day that @140journos went to work was two days before the OdaTV case, on the anniversary of the murder of Hrant Dink (see page 24). Engin Önder: 'In the initial phase we ourselves were the people placing the content on the Twitter account. We went to demonstrations, commemorations, court cases, you name it, and tweeted what we saw happening, up until the demonstrations for Gezi Park in the spring of 2013. To be honest, at the time we were already starting to lose enthusiasm for @140journos, as there was little development. But civic journalism suddenly blossomed as a result of the Gezi protests. Gezi demonstrators began tweeting content to us. Then we decided we would no longer focus on creating content ourselves, but on checking information reaching us from others on Twitter.'

So the Twitter account not only has a lot of its own followers, but also follows roughly 15,000 people. Önder: 'We also have a lot of activist friends keeping us up to date on where they are. For example we know whether Meltem is going to a demonstration against mining or hydro power stations, or where people on Twitter who we follow are reporting from. We never simply re-tweet. There are always several people tweeting from a demonstration, and we compare their reports, so that you get a good complete picture of what's going on.'

In addition, @140journos makes use of all kinds of technology to check information: they Google photographs to see whether they have been used before, zoom in on locations on Google Maps, check whether photographs have been Photoshopped, you name it. No matter how

journalistically @140journos approaches its work, for years Önder refused
to call himself a journalist. He explains: 'It's a bit of a dirty word because
in Turkey journalism has been used the way it is being used now – for
power. The news media take no responsibility for their reporting, they
allow themselves to be bought readily and thus become a government
instrument. News media are commerce, and the right of the people to be
informed takes second place. This has always been the case, it even goes
back to the Ottoman period.'

He is now calling himself a journalist, even if it is one of the many
things that he does. He earns his living with his advertising agency Yaratici
Fikirler Enstitusu, the Institute of Creative Minds. The editorial team
of @140journos has now grown to eight volunteers and the occasional
intern. No, not taken from journalism academies in Turkey – they are
categorically rejected. Önder says: 'They are too attached to what they learn
in school and it does not connect with what we are doing. We would rather
have interns studying international relations, politics or history.' Those
new to the crew make the occasional mistake', Önder says. For example,
somebody turned the PYD Kurdish party in Syria into the PDY instead.
Önder: 'We got angry reactions, even though a typing error like that is not
deliberate.'

In June 2015 @140journos made another major change: they now also
tweet news from newspapers and news agencies, and they also attempt
to check these sources, because they turn out to be not always reliable –
something that does not surprise him. These include Turkey's largest news
agencies Anadolu Ajans (linked to the state and fully under the control of
the AKP) and DHA (from the Dogan stable), and also the Kurdish bureaus
ANF (Firat News Agency) and DIHA (Dicle News Agency), as well as all
sorts of websites putting out their own news. Önder says: 'In the end, you
can't follow events in a country using only civic journalism. For that there
is just too much going on in Turkey.'

Since then @140journos has very occasionally made a mistake.
For example, OdaTV put out that former President Abdullah Gül's name

had been removed from the list of AKP founders on the AKP website. 'We put that out as well, but it turned out not to be true. We removed it and published a correction. Other news media did the same, but the news is still on many websites.'

Another more embarrassing mistake was the news from DIHA that an 11-year-old boy had been killed in violence in south-eastern Turkey. The news was distributed by the news agency with a photograph. @140journos checked the photograph that had not been used elsewhere and saw the report as reliable enough to put out. 'But then there was a report from the boy's family stating that none of their children had died,' Önder says. 'The news had also suddenly disappeared from the DIHA website. We were extremely embarrassed and corrected the story. Our reputation is so strong, and it may not be harmed.'

But checking the news is increasingly problematic, certainly in the Kurdish south-east of the country, where violence has soared over recent months and where 24-hour curfews are in force in many cities and districts. Önder: 'If no one can go out onto the street, you are also unable to follow several sources from the scene on Twitter to check the reports. What do you do in that case? We said that we would share this dilemma faced by our editors with our followers. We put out what DIHA publishes, and also what Anadolu has to say about it.'

The strong reputation of @140journos for reliability ensures that it is followed by Twitter users of all backgrounds and political preferences and has scarcely any difficulties with trolls jamming the @140journos account with spam or abuse. 'This means that there still a lot of people in this country who simply want to hear the bare facts. They don't get them anywhere else. The famous 'AKP trolls' don't attack us either. They follow us. People re-tweet our facts and add their own comments.'

Has he had offers over the years from people who saw money in @140journos and wanted to invest in the account? 'Not once,' Önder says, adding: 'Nobody wants to invest in journalism.'

_ Haci Bogatekin, founder and editor of the local newspaper Gerger Firat: 'Journalism brings us sorrow'

From 1976 to 1992 Haci Bogatekin worked for the press bureau of the country's largest newspaper, Hürriyet, in Gerger, the town where he was born in 1950. At the time, Gerger and the more than 40 surrounding villages had a population of around 30,000. Things started to go wrong, Bogatekin writes in an email, when Hürriyet was taken over by the Dogan empire in 1992. 'During the time that Sedat Simavi was Hürriyet's owner, before 1992, journalism took pride of place. Once it was in Dogan's hands commerce took over. And especially news from reporters in cities where many of Dogan's advertisers were based. Gerger was a small place without companies that advertised. We wrote up news stories and sent them in, but the head office never published them and threw our copy into the wastepaper basket.' But he writes: 'I'm a journalist to the core. I was, you could say, a news machine. In order to publish my news in freedom, I then set up Gerger Firat.'

He has never struggled to fill its pages. Bogatekin: 'Gerger is small, but there is a lot going on and there are major problems. To point out one example, young people are leaving Gerger, with the result that older people are left without care and with difficulties, and that has consequences for the community. Without a decent newspaper, people are not kept informed about this.'

In 1994, as Bogatekin puts it, 'the heavy traffic of legal cases began'. Since then a total of as many as 160 cases have been opened against him. He has been jailed several times and has heard demands for sentences totalling decades in prison. Many of the cases are ongoing, while some convictions have been dismissed by higher courts, and he has in fact been imprisoned on various occasions – for the first time following the 1980 military coup. He was accused of insulting an army colonel and was sentenced to seven months in jail, serving five.

During those years the military authorities began to make life difficult for him in all sorts of other ways too. Bogatekin: 'In 1982 the police attacked me because I was filming a disturbance at the market in Gerger. Before that they had come into the office, smashed my typewriter to pieces on the ground, destroyed my camera and confiscated my files. They also locked and sealed the office for 30 days.'

And that was not the end of it, he says. 'I once published a piece about the municipality's poor refuse collection service that resulted in the streets often being dirty. The water to my house was immediately cut and I received a fine from the water company. Following a story about the many cuts in the electricity supply, the power to both my home and the office was cut. A fine from the electricity company followed, and a court case in which I was accused of tapping off electricity illegally. I got 11 months, but the sentence was reversed on appeal.'

The 'biggest legal blow' came in 2008, following publication of alleged links between the public prosecutor in Gerger and the movement of Fethullah Gülen. He wrote that the greatest danger came not from the PKK, but from the Gülen movement, referring to PKK leader Öcalan as 'Apo' and Gülen as 'Feto'. Bogatekin was detained and held for almost four months.

The conviction was handed down two years later: five years in prison. His crime: defamation, slander and perverting the course of justice. Bogatekin's son, Özgür, who had started working for his father's newspaper, was also given a prison sentence: one year, two months and 17 days for 'intervening against police use of force'. Haci Bogatekin says: 'As a result of amendments to the law in 2013, I have not yet had to serve the sentence. But I can still be ordered to prison at any time.'

Bogatekin has for long had neither the time nor the money to attend all the cases and appeals, which in Turkey can drag on for years. He writes in his email: 'I go only if the case is in Gerger, otherwise the travel costs mount up too much. But I can't appoint any lawyers, and if I'm not there, there is no one to defend me.'

Then he is facing a number of cases in which various official people are demanding compensation for damages from him. He summarises: 'A governor is demanding 20,000 lira, two members of parliament each 10,000 lira, another governor 10,000 lira. My income? I barely earn anything from the newspaper, and I have a monthly pension of 1,100 lira (€342, £264). I have 12 children, one of whom is still studying, while the others are married or working. I do not own my house, or a car, and haven't got a cent in the bank.'

Reporters Without Borders is supporting Bogatekin through his many court cases and intimidation, but the local journalist often feels that he is invisible among all the press freedom cases in Turkey that receive a great deal of national and international attention. He writes: 'Right up to today we are providing extremely serious journalism. But it is as if we remain a shrub in the shadow of the big trees.'

However, there is certainly respect within the profession in Turkey. In 2008 Haci Bogatekin was awarded the Press Freedom Award by the Turkish Journalists' Society, and in 2009 he was acknowledged by the Contemporary Journalists' Association.

When I read Bogatekin's email I ask myself whether he does in fact represent 'hope'. How far do you go for journalism? Do you allow your life to be totally disrupted by it, do you allow yourself to be financially destroyed? Is that hope? Pure stubbornness? Is it worth it?

But then the email takes a surprising turn. Haci Bogatekin writes that his newspaper 'is a bridge between Gerger and the people who have left'. Gerger Firat has 3,000 paying subscribers – a lot for a local newspaper in Turkey – and he uses his subscribers and his unmatched network to do good. He continues: 'Since 1996 there has been an aid bridge between Gerger and Istanbul, where many people from Gerger went. People from Istanbul donate for schools and students, and in Gerger we distribute it.' There was another major collection campaign at the beginning of 2016.

Bogatekin says: 'We throw all the stress that journalism has brought us into the aid campaigns. Journalism causes us sorrow, but I love our work helping schoolchildren. You know, Ms Fréderike, Gerger is small. There is no lawyer, no foundation or association, nothing. There are no other newspapers, no other journalists, and we are not even politically represented. The load weighing down on the shoulders of the journalist is a heavy one.'

HALIT GÜNGEN (1971-1992)

This young investigative journalist was murdered on 18 February 1992, two days after his story on collaboration between the Turkish army and Hezbollah militants was published by the magazine 2000'e Dogru (After 2000). Born into a family of 10 children in the south-eastern province of Sirnak, Güngen was the son of a father who eked out a living as farmer and construction worker. Halit Güngen was found dead in his office in the south-eastern city of Diyarbakir, where he worked as full-time correspondent for 2000'e Dogru.

In his story Güngen provided evidence that he had uncovered collaboration between the Turkish army and Hezbollah (not linked to the Lebanese Hezbollah), a group that committed a series of murders of mostly Kurdish writers, journalists, politicians, intellectuals and activists in the south-east of Turkey during the 1990s. Hezbollah was set up following the 1980 military coup and was used by the state during the 1990s in its war against the PKK. Hezbollah may even have been set up by the state – at least many of those involved have alleged this in subsequent court cases.

Not much was known about Hezbollah at the time of Güngen's article. Güngen had uncovered that Hezbollah was being controlled by Turkey's MIT security service, and that Hezbollah members trained at a riot squad camp in Diyarbakir Province. He knew some of the names of the Hezbollah members who were attending the courses, and the days on which they were to be found at the base. Güngen received threats while carrying out his investigations, but he persisted nevertheless, deciding to publish the results under the headline 'Hezbollah being trained at riot police base'. 2000'e Dogru, which no longer exists, was a significant magazine at the time, with a print run of between 20,000 and 25,000 copies. Hezbollah was discussed widely in Turkey for the first time as a consequence of the story.

There was no progress in the investigation into the murder for the first eight years. That changed in 2000, when the trial began in Diyarbakir of 31 alleged Hezbollah members suspected of as many as 188 murders, including that of Halit Güngen. Cemal Tutar was alleged to have been Güngen's murderer. He received a life sentence along with 16 others in 2009. The case was referred to a higher court. Pending a final verdict many of those convicted, including Cemal Tutar, were released on 3 January 2011, as the maximum term for being held on remand had expired. When a judge issued an arrest warrant for those released 11 days later they were nowhere to be found. The 'life' sentence handed down to 16 of those convicted was confirmed later that month on 26 January, but they remain at large.

The magazine 2000'e Dogru ceased to exist in 1992 after five years of publication. Mecit Akgün, another journalist on the magazine, was murdered that year. In June his body was found hanging from a telephone poll in a village in Mardin Province in south-eastern Turkey with a note pinned to it saying that he had been 'punished for treason'. The PKK was said to be responsible, but the murder has never been cleared up, let alone anyone punished for it.

IZZET KEZER (1954-1992)

Kezer began his career as a journalist at the major national newspaper Sabah in 1988. On 21 March 1992 he travelled to Cizre in the south-east to cover Newroz, the Kurdish New Year. A curfew was imposed in the city two days after Newroz, during which Kezer was shot by the security forces.

The 1992 Newroz celebrations erupted in many towns and cities in the south-east into the so-called 'Serhildan', a rebellion by the Kurdish population against vastly increased use of force by the state in the region. The Serdilhan was fuelled in part by the death in February of Cengiz Altun, a reporter for the Kurdish Yeni Ülke (New Country), in Batman Province in the south-east. Cizre residents wanted during Newroz to go to the cemetery where PKK fighters are among those buried, but the police opened fire on the crowd, killing 11. Newroz erupted into violence in other towns as well, and almost 100 people died in total. Following Newroz, the authorities imposed a curfew on 23 March. Faruk Balikci, a journalist who reports from Diyarbakir to this day, was there along with Izzet Kezer and a few other fellow journalists. He told the independent Bianet.org portal how they were sitting in a hotel when they heard a child screaming. They left the hotel with a group of 10 journalists to see where the screaming was coming from. 'Shots were fired, and we sought cover in buildings,' Balikci said. 'We made three white flags so that we could go back onto the road. I carried one, Izzet another, and a German journalist took one. We went up the road again, and again multiple shots were fired. We sought cover in iron doorways. When we looked around afterwards, we saw that Izzet had been hit in the head and was lying in a pool of blood.'

It took half an hour before the group was able to recover their dead colleague from where he was lying in the road, as they came under fire every time they tried to reach the body. The prosecutor came to the hotel the same day to take statements from the witnesses, but Balikci told independent news portal Bianet.org years later: 'I said I did not believe that who had fired the shots would ever come out and that the perpetrators would never be identified; that the investigation was merely a formality. And indeed, we never heard any more about it.'

Balikci added: 'Izzet's dossier states that the cartridge case was never found and that the perpetrator is unknown. But on that day there was no one on the street. Everyone was indoors. One of our colleagues who remained behind was fired on in a small backstreet from an army vehicle, but he was able to take cover by hiding behind a truck.' In August 1992, referring to the many journalists murdered, the then prime minister Demirel said: 'Those who were murdered were not genuine journalists. They were militants disguised as journalists. They murdered each other.' In January 1993, a couple of months later, Minister Mehmet Battalli said that Izzet Kezer had been the only journalist murdered in the Kurdish south-east. However, the murder has never been solved.

ACKNOWLEDGEMENTS

'A book on press freedom in Turkey – that will certainly be a very thin little book!' I was told on innumerable occasions when I let slip that I was busy with this undertaking. However, the topic is so big, and hides so many complex mechanisms, that I was at first completely tied up in knots by it. How should I write about it in such a way as to make it intelligible to people who know little or nothing at all about Turkey? How do I make clear that while the lack of press freedom has been taken to extreme lengths in the Turkey of President Erdogan, the problem lies much deeper than one man alone? Conversations with Bilge Yesil, Associate Professor of Media Culture at the City University of New York, and with Erol Önderoglu, Turkey representative of Journalists Without Borders, helped me to order my thoughts. Thanks to both of you!

I express my gratitude of course to all the people to whom I spoke over the months and years on this topic and who are quoted in this booklet: Hüseyin Aykol (Özgür Gündem editor), Amberin Zaman (freelance journalist), Yasemin Congar (formerly at Taraf, now T24), Can Dündar (Cumhuriyet editor), Haci Bogatekin (founder and editor of Gerger Firat), Bülent Kenes (Today's Zaman, until the newspaper was taken over by the government), Erdal Güven (co-founder and editor of Diken.com.tr) and Engin Önder (co-founder and the brain behind the Twitter account @140journos). My thanks to the T24 legal team for helping to disentangle a couple of constitutional issues.

Rudolf Geel and Jan Honout of the Eva Tas Foundation: my thanks for your extreme patience and rock-solid confidence.

Fréderike Geerdink
Leiden, March 2016

SAFYETTIN TEPE (1968-1995)

Safyettin Tepe was Batman correspondent for the magazine Yeni Politika (New Politics). At the end of August 1995 he was detained in Batman to be transferred to the counter-terrorism police bureau in the neighbouring province of Bitlis. Four days later he was dead. The police insisted he had hanged himself in his cell, but the circumstances surrounding his death have never been brought to light.

Safyettin decided to be a journalist in 1993, inspired by his nephew Ferhat Tepe, a cub reporter who had been abducted and murdered in Turkey's Kurdish southeast. The Tepe family believes that Ferhat was murdered by the police, but the case has never been cleared up. Much like Ferhat, Safyettin began his career working for the Kurdish newspaper Özgür Gündem in Agri, Adana and Gaziantep, later moving to Yeni Politika, a publication from the same stable as Özgür Gündem.

Safyettin's elder brother Tayyip told the independent news portal bianet.org that he had talked to his brother shortly before he was arrested. The authorities were on the point of banning Yeni Politika, and the two brothers spoke about what Safyettin could do as a journalist after it was shut down. Tayyip: 'On 23 August the police came to the offices of Özgür Gündem in Istanbul to enquire about Safyettin. When they realised that he was in Batman, the newspaper staff phoned Safyettin to say that the police were looking for him, but my brother seemed to be unconcerned. Two days later he was detained along with two colleagues. The other two were soon released, but not Safyettin.'

The official autopsy report stated that Safyettin had hanged himself using his undershirt. The family refused to believe this and requested that a second autopsy be carried out, but the police refused to grant permission. Initially the police also did not want to return Safyettin's body to the family, but his father nevertheless prevailed. Safyettin's feet and back were black and blue, and there were blue marks on his head. There were only slight marks around his neck, which certainly did not make the official autopsy any more credible.

The family's efforts to have a thorough investigation opened into Sefyettin's death had no success. A decision was taken in 1996 that there was no reason to refer the matter to a court, as Safyettin Tepe had hanged himself in his cell with his undershirt. In fact this shirt has never been found, and according to his family, Safyettin never wore an undershirt.

The family took the case to the European Court of Human Rights (ECHR). In 2004 the ECHR ruled that the case had been submitted too late. All domestic legal avenues have to be exhausted before the ECHR will consider a case, and the Tepe family evidently realised only too late that the ECHR imposes a time limit. By the time they made application to the ECHR it was too late.

PREVIOUSLY APPEARED IN THE SERIES

_ Honduras _ Dina Meza, *Kidnapped*
_ Vietnam _ Bui Thanh Hieu, *Speaking in Silence*
_ China _ Sofie Sun, *Drugs for the Mind*
_ Ethiopia _ Bisrat Handiso, *Genocide of Thought*
_ Macedonia _ Tomislav Kezharovski, *Likvidacija/Annihilation*

TO APPEAR SPRING 2016

_ Cuba _ Amir Valle, *Gagged*
_ Cuba _ Amir Valle, *Palabras Amordazadas*
_ Bangladesh _ Parvez Alam, *Disappearing Public Spheres*
_ Turkey _ Fréderike Geerdink, *Bans, Jails and Shameless Lies*
_ Economics _ Peter de Haan, *Censorship Alert*

TO APPEAR AUTUMN 2016

_ El Salvador _ Jorge Galán, *The Long Shadow*
_ Surinam _ Sylvana van den Braak, *A Fri Wortu*

The printed titles are available for free via
Janhonout@evatasfoundation.com.
As an ebook via the common outlets.

www.ingramcontent.com/pod-product-compliance
Lightning Source LLC
Chambersburg PA
CBHW071347290326
41933CB00041B/2897